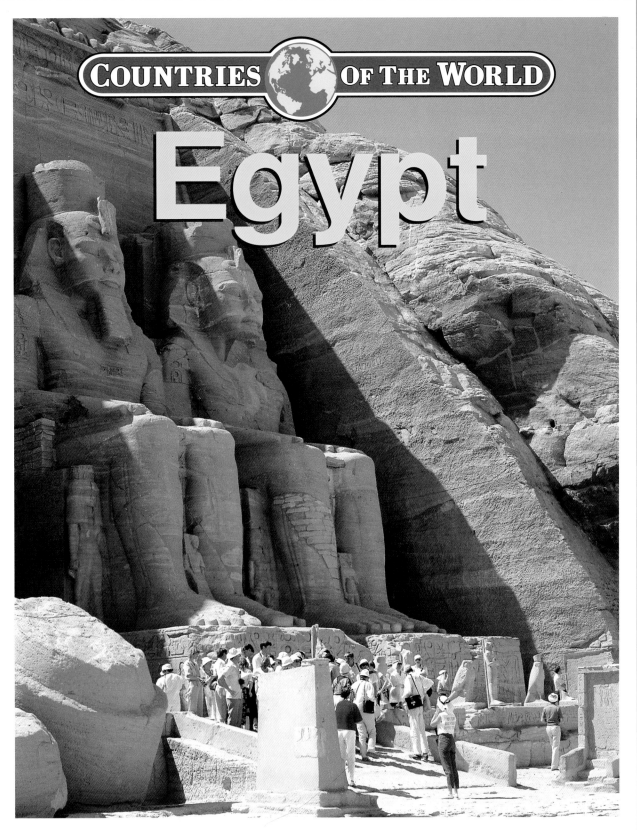

COUNTRIES OF THE WORLD

Egypt

Gareth Stevens Publishing
MILWAUKEE

About the Author: Dr. Susan L. Wilson studied anthropology at Southern Methodist University and the University of Cincinnati. She has been conducting research in Egypt for over ten years and has taught for many years.

Written by
SUSAN L. WILSON

Edited by
JUNIA BAKER

Designed by
JAILANI BASARI

Picture research by
SUSAN JANE MANUEL

First published in North America in 1999 by
Gareth Stevens Publishing
1555 North RiverCenter Drive, Suite 201
Milwaukee, Wisconsin 53212 USA

For a free color catalog describing
Gareth Stevens' list of high-quality books
and multimedia programs, call
1-800-542-2595 (USA) or
1-800-461-9120 (CANADA).
Gareth Stevens Publishing's
Fax: (414) 225-0377.
See our catalog, too, on the World Wide Web:
gsinc.com

© **TIMES EDITIONS PTE LTD 1999**
Originated and designed by
Times Books International
an imprint of Times Editions Pte Ltd
Times Centre, 1 New Industrial Road
Singapore 536196
http://www.timesone.com.sg/te

Library of Congress Cataloging-in-Publication Data
Wilson, Susan L. (Susan Louise), 1947–
Egypt / [Susan L. Wilson].
p.   cm. -- (Countries of the world)
Includes bibliographical references (p. 94) and index.
Summary: An overview of Egypt, including an in-depth section on a variety of topics that make the country unique.
ISBN 0-8368-2259-5 (lib. bdg.)
1. Egypt--Juvenile literature. [1. Egypt.] I. Title.
II. Series: Countries of the world (Milwaukee, Wis.)
DT49.W57   1998
962--dc21   98-35852

Printed in Singapore

1 2 3 4 5 6 7 8 9 03 02 01 00 99

Contents

AN OVERVIEW OF EGYPT

Egypt brings to mind visions of pyramids, grand temples, gigantic monuments, mummies, and king-gods, all relics of one of the oldest civilizations in the world. It is called the "Land of the Pharaohs," a place where agriculture and advanced mathematics both flourished. The long reign of pharaohs (FAIR-ohs) and grand monuments, however, passed away nearly two thousand years ago. Many facets of life in Egypt have changed since that time.

Egypt (formally, the Arab Republic of Egypt) is an Arab nation in Africa. The official language is Arabic. The capital city is Cairo, or el Qahirah (el KA-heh-rah). Egypt covers 386,662 square miles (1,001,455 square kilometers).

Opposite: **The Temple of Karnak was built in the twentieth century B.C. It is in Luxor, which is about 400 miles (640 km) south of Cairo.**

Below: **Welcome from the children of Egypt:** *ahlan wa sahlan* **(AH-lan was-AH-lan)!**

THE FLAG OF EGYPT

The tradition of flags actually began in ancient Egypt and Assyria. Sacred objects were mounted on poles as rallying points for battle or symbols of royal authority. The flag of modern Egypt was first used after the 1952 revolution against British rule. The white stands for a bright future, the black for a dark past, and the red for the revolution. In the center is the golden eagle of Salladin, a Syrian army officer who drove invaders out of Egypt in 1169 and then made himself Egypt's ruler. The eagle replaced an earlier symbol of a hawk.

Geography

Egypt is in the northeastern corner of Africa and connects Africa with Asia and Europe. The Mediterranean Sea lies on Egypt's northern boundary. The Gaza Strip, Israel, and the Red Sea are to the east. Libya shares Egypt's western border, and Sudan is on the southern border.

Egypt is overwhelmingly a desert country divided by the Nile River. The Western (Libyan) Desert is the largest, covering 262,800 square miles (680,652 square km). It is part of the Sahara Desert, which extends across much of northern Africa. The landscape is primarily bare rocks and sandy plains. The Eastern (Arabian) Desert lies east of the Nile. There is little vegetation except for some brushy plants along the *wadis* (WAD-ees), or dry stream beds. The sands are a golden color with a hint of red, reflecting the minerals in the limestone deposits. A chain of rugged mountains borders the desert along the Red Sea coast.

Below: **The Western Desert is a flat, sandy plateau. It is part of the Sahara Desert, which crosses much of northern Africa, from the Nile Valley to the Atlantic Ocean.**

The Sinai Peninsula in northeastern Egypt is a sand desert. In the south, rising high above the Red Sea coast, are spectacular granite mountains, some reaching over 8,000 feet (2,438 meters). Mount Catherine is the highest, at 8,668 feet (2,642 m). The middle region is a plateau, with valleys gradually descending to the Mediterranean Sea. The northern region is a plain where rain waters from the southern and middle areas of the peninsula gather.

The Nile River cuts a snaky path through Egypt's vast desert plateau, giving the country its major source of fresh water. The Nile is the longest river in the world, flowing 4,132 miles (6,648 km) from south to north. It starts from the distant headwaters of the White Nile deep in central Africa and empties into the Mediterranean Sea. The Blue Nile, which begins in the highlands of Ethiopia, converges with the White Nile in Khartoum, Sudan, to form the Nile River. Just north of Cairo, the Nile branches into a wide delta.

Heavy rains in central Africa cause the Nile to rise every year. Until flood control measures were taken by building dams in Aswan, the river flooded its banks annually. The world's largest artificial lake, Lake Nasser, was created behind the Aswan High Dam, which became operational in 1970.

Above: **Marine life in the Red Sea includes stingrays; reef sharks; sponges; dolphins; turtles; and mollusks, such as clams, bivalves, and oysters. Both hard and soft coral animals also live in the Red Sea, and at least a thousand species of fish have been identified there.**

IRRIGATION

Farmland has been irrigated for many years through a system of canals. Before the flooding of the Nile was controlled by dams, measuring sticks called nilometers were used to tell when the Nile was rising and when it was time to open the channels to the irrigation canals.
(A Closer Look, page 56)

Seasons

Egypt has only two seasons: a hot season and a cool season. The climate is dry with very low humidity. Temperatures and humidity can be very different in Alexandria on the Mediterranean Sea compared to the desert in southern Egypt. The hot season, May to October, is followed by a cool, mild winter from November to April. Winter temperatures throughout Egypt average 55° to 70° Fahrenheit (13° to 21° Centigrade). Summer temperatures can reach as high as 122° to 126° F (50° to 52° C) in the southern desert but tend to stay much cooler along the Mediterranean coast.

Egypt has very little rainfall. Areas along the Mediterranean coast receive about 8 inches (20 centimeters) of rain each year, but in Aswan, the average is less than 0.5 inches (1.3 cm) every five years.

Above: **Dates are the most common fruit in Egypt. Date palms grow throughout the country.**

Left: **Although much of Egypt is a flat desert, barren mountains range from north to south along the Red Sea coast and the banks of the Nile.**

Plants and Animals

Egypt has about a hundred species of mammals, more than four hundred species of birds, thirty-four species of snakes, many lizards and insects, and an amazing abundance of marine life. The most common large mammals are camels, donkeys, water buffalo, cattle, sheep, goats, and horses. House mice, rats, and bats far outnumber the large mammals.

About one-third of the birds sighted in Egypt actually breed there. Each year, one to two million birds pass through Egypt as they migrate from Europe to Africa. Many large birds, such as storks, flamingos, cranes, and herons, are protected by Egyptian law. Falcons, eagles, vultures, hawks, egrets, and owls are the main birds of prey. The ibis, a sacred bird worshiped by ancient Egyptians as the living image of their god, Thoth, can be found in Sudan but is extinct in Egypt.

Egypt's desert environment limits most vegetation to the Nile Valley, the delta, and the oases. The lotus and papyrus plants have been symbols of Egypt since ancient times. Egypt's most common native tree is the date palm. Other trees include the sycamore, tamarisk, and carob. Halfa grass and thorn trees grow in desert regions. Another common plant is the water hyacinth, or Nile Rose. Cotton, sugarcane, corn, tomatoes, wheat, rice, citrus fruits, and potatoes are Egypt's most important commercial crops.

CLOTHES AND VEILS

One of the most interesting weather phenomena in Egypt is the *khamsin* (KAHMA-SEEN). A khamsin is a hot, dry wind with sandstorms that blows in from the Western Desert during April and May. Khamsin winds not only damage crops but can cause difficulties for people breathing the dusty air. The traditional long clothing, scarves, and veils worn by many Egyptians provide protection from the wind.

(A Closer Look, page 46)

Left: The poisonous banded *Naja haje annulifera,* or Egyptian cobra, is about 6 feet (2 m) long and preys on toads and birds.

History

The earliest indications of humans in the Nile Valley date from about 250,000 B.C. in the area of Upper Egypt and Nubia. These people were Old Stone Age, or Paleolithic people. Toward the end of this period (about 25,000 B.C.), the climate in Egypt changed drastically, turning the grassy plains into desert. By the Middle Stone Age, or Mesolithic era (about 10,000–5000 B.C.), a number of groups lived in Egypt and made their living as semi-nomadic fishers and hunters. During the New Stone Age, or Neolithic period (about 5000–3400 B.C.), the people became more sedentary. They grew cereal crops, had primitive shelters, made pottery, and had tools and weapons made of flint.

LAND OF THE GODS

The original people of Nubia lived in the area between Aswan in the south of Egypt and Khartoum in Sudan. The area was called Kush, later Ethiopia.
(A Closer Look, page 60)

Left: The Sphinx, with the head of a man and the body of a lion, stands as guardian over the Great Pyramids, one of the seven ancient wonders of the world.

10

Above: **Tourists line up to enter the pyramid of Khufu.**

The next major period in Egyptian history was the Predynastic period (c. 3400–3100 B.C.). By the end of this period, there was evidence of two competing groups headed by leaders who were called kings, or pharaohs. During the Early Dynastic period (c. 3100–2686 B.C.), Menes (MEE-neez), the ruler of Upper Egypt, conquered Lower Egypt and established a united kingdom in the Nile Valley at Memphis (close to Cairo). Thirty dynasties followed (the Old Kingdom, the Middle Kingdom, and the New Kingdom) until the invasion in 330 B.C. by Alexander the Great.

The Ptolemaic dynasty followed Alexander's death and stayed in power until 31 B.C., when the Romans defeated Egypt's fleets under Queen Cleopatra VII. Egypt became part of the Roman empire and adopted Christianity in A.D. 312.

When the Arabs invaded Egypt in 639, they brought their Islamic religion, which has since been a major formative influence in the development of modern Egyptian society. Large numbers of Arabs followed the invasion, settled in the Nile Valley, and gradually became the majority of the population.

The Mamluks (MAHM-lukes), former Arab slaves, established a dynasty from 1250 to 1517. This lasted until Egypt became a province of the Ottoman Empire. The Ottomans ruled Egypt until French General Napoleon Bonaparte led an expedition to Egypt in 1798. The British and French both wanted control of Egypt, but the British took over with the help of the Ottomans.

GIFT OF THE NILE

During the Old Kingdom (c. 2686–2181 B.C.), Egypt's famous pyramids at Giza were built as tombs for Pharaohs Khufu, Khafre, and Menkaure. Each block of stone weighed about two and a half tons and was transported to the site by boat when the Nile River flooded each year.
(A Closer Look, page 54)

Modern History

Egypt acquired partial independence from Britain in February 1922. At the end of World War I, Egypt's nationalist leaders had formed an organization called Wafd (WAH-fed), which is the Arabic word for delegation, and presented their demands for complete independence. The British said the Egyptians were "not ready" for self-government, so the Wafd organized strikes, boycotts, and terrorist attacks against British soldiers and Egyptians who were thought to be on the British side. The British abolished the protectorate in 1922, but refused to give up control over Egyptian foreign policy, defense, and communications. The new government was a constitutional monarchy with a king and a parliament, but Egypt was still not in control of all its affairs.

Great Britain took full control over Egypt again during World War II because Britain needed a military base in the Mediterranean and was afraid that Germany would take over the Suez Canal. When the British reinstated the protectorate, one of Egypt's greatest leaders, Gamal Abdel Nasser, said that the action aroused in him the seeds of revolt. "It made [us] realize that there is a dignity to be retrieved and defended." On July 23, 1952, the Free Officers, a secret organization, launched the Egyptian revolution.

FIGHTS WITH NEIGHBORS

When Israel was established in 1948, the Palestinians lost part of their homeland. There were clashes between Israel and the surrounding countries, including Egypt, especially after Israel occupied all of Palestine and parts of Egypt and Syria.
(A Closer Look, page 52)

Below: Victory parade for the October 1973 war that President Sadat launched against Israel to convince Israel to negotiate for peace with its Arab neighbors.

In 1954, Nasser became the republic's president, prime minister, and head of the Revolutionary Command Council. He is most noted for reforming Egypt's economy into a centrally planned, socialist model; attempting to establish a Pan-Arab alliance; developing close ties with the Soviet Union; building the Aswan High Dam; and nationalizing the Suez Canal.

Nasser remained president until he died in 1970. He was succeeded by Vice President Anwar al-Sadat. In 1972, Sadat ordered all Soviet advisors out of Egypt to reduce Egypt's dependence on the Soviets and to bridge an alliance with the United States. This alliance was set back when Egypt launched an offensive against Israel in 1973 to liberate occupied Sinai. The offensive also made Israel willing to negotiate for peace, which led to the Camp David Accords.

On October 6, 1981, President Sadat was killed by assassins who belonged to secret groups that advocated the establishment of a pure Islamic society in Egypt. They accused Sadat of favoring Western capitalism, of making peace with the "enemy of Islam" (Israel), and of not being a good Muslim.

Following the assassination, Vice President Mohammed Hosni Mubarak became the next president. He has become an advocate for peace in the Middle East, which continues to be an important issue in the world today.

Above: **Al Faisal of Saudi Arabia *(center)* and Farouk al Sharaa of Syria *(left)* meet with President Hosni Mubarak of Egypt *(right)*. Mubarak has become known for creating good relationships with Egypt's neighbors.**

PEACE WITH ISRAEL

The ongoing conflict with Israel was finally settled in 1979. Israeli Prime Minister Menachem Begin and Egyptian President Anwar al-Sadat met for negotiations at Camp David in the United States, at the invitation of U.S. President Jimmy Carter. A peace treaty was signed on March 26, 1979.

(A Closer Look, page 62)

13

Ramses II (Nineteenth Dynasty)

Ramses II was one of several generals who ruled Egypt during the nineteenth and twentieth dynasties. During his reign, and between waging war against the Libyans and Hittites, he and his successors built a great number of buildings in Thebes, now known as Luxor. They competed with each other in building great temples on the eastern side of the Nile and even greater mortuary temples on the western side, all in the name of the ancient god Amun.

Above: **The obelisk and head of Ramses II in Luxor.**

Queen Hatshepsut (Eighteenth Dynasty)

Hatshepsut, who reigned as queen of Egypt between 1503 and 1458 B.C., was the daughter of Thutmosis I. She married Thutmosis II, her half-brother and heir to the throne. When her husband died, Hatshepsut shared the throne with Thutmosis III, her husband's heir but had herself declared pharaoh and excluded Thutmosis III from political power during her lifetime. Hatshepsut was the only female pharaoh. Her twenty-year reign was a time of peace and growth in Egypt.

Above: President Gamal Abdel Nasser ruled Egypt from 1954 until he died in 1970. He was one of the architects of the Nonaligned Movement, countries that distanced themselves from both Western and communist political powers and wanted to be a third force in world politics.

Muhammad 'Ali Pasha (1769–1849)

Many consider Muhammad 'Ali Pasha to be the true founder of modern Egypt. He established the dynasty that ruled Egypt from the beginning of the nineteenth century to the middle of the twentieth century. When he became viceroy and pasha (governor) in 1805, he confiscated all private lands, built an administrative system similar to the present-day's, instituted educational and training programs, opened new factories, and built a canal between Alexandria and the Nile River.

Gamal Abdel Nasser (1918–1970)

After World War II, Gamal Abdel Nasser and his fellow officers were determined to overthrow the monarchy and end the British protectorate. They launched a revolution on July 23, 1952, and in 1954, Nasser became president, prime minister, and head of the Revolutionary Command Council. He reformed Egypt's economy on a socialist model, built the Aswan High Dam, and nationalized the Suez Canal.

President Anwar al-Sadat *(above)*, along with Prime Minister Menachem Begin of Israel, received the Nobel Peace Prize in 1978 for stabilizing relations between Israel and Egypt.

Anwar al-Sadat (1918–1981)

Muhammad Anwar al-Sadat succeeded Nasser as president. He is remembered most for securing peace between Egypt and Israel, but he also developed an open-door economic policy by aligning his country with the West, seeking out Western assistance and technology, and bringing an end to Nasser's socialist system of government. Sadat was assassinated on October 6, 1981.

Government and the Economy

Egypt adopted its permanent constitution on September 11, 1971, and subsequently amended it on May 22, 1980. Egypt's government is a democratic republic ruled by a president. Mohammed Hosni Mubarak, the current president, took office in 1981, when the preceding president, Anwar al-Sadat, was assassinated. Mubarak was reelected in 1987.

The head of the government is the prime minister, appointed by the president. The prime minister's cabinet, or his ministers, is also appointed by the president. The country is divided into twenty-six administrative units, or governorates, each of which is divided into cities and villages. The cities and villages are also administrative units and are considered corporate bodies.

The government consists of legislative, executive, and judicial branches, along with the Shura Consultative Council, or advisory council, which is partially elected. Egypt's legislative branch consists of the People's Assembly, which has considerable power to supervise the executive branch, approve state policy and the budget, and propose laws. The People's Assembly has no fewer than 350 elected members, at least half of whom are required to be ordinary people chosen by a secret, public vote. The president may appoint up to ten members to the Assembly. As of 1998,

Below: Voters turn out for elections. Every citizen over the age of eighteen is required to vote.

Above: **The Egyptian government helps the poor with health care, free education, and government-run child care centers.**

there are 454 Members of the Assembly. The president convenes each session of the Assembly.

Executive power resides with the president, who is head of state. The People's Assembly nominates the president and then refers him to the people for a referendum vote. The candidate is elected president after receiving an absolute majority of votes cast in the election. The president may be elected to an unlimited number of six-year terms.

Judicial decisions in Egypt are made by judges, not juries. Egyptian judges are independent, subject to no other authority than the law, and have an international reputation for conducting fair trials.

The Shura Consultative Council supports all sections of the government but does not have any real authority. The concept of an advisory committee comes from an age-old Muslim tradition in which the local village leaders hear concerns, recommend actions, and settle disputes. The Council has 264 seats, 176 elected and 88 appointed by the president.

Egypt has a multi-party political system. There is a constitutional ban on religious-based political parties. Even so, the technically illegal group, the Muslim Brotherhood, has some influence in Egypt.

EMERGENCY LAW

Under the Emergency Law (in effect since 1981), cases involving terrorism and national security may be tried in military or state security courts. In these cases, the accused does not receive all the constitutional protections people have in the judicial system. Use of the Emergency Law has come under attack by many international human rights organizations.

Economy

Egypt's main sources of income are from the Suez Canal, agriculture, textiles, food processing, tourism, chemicals, petroleum, construction, cement, and metals. Its main exports are petroleum and petroleum products, cotton, cotton textiles and clothing, farm produce, and aluminum products. Its main trading partners are France, Greece, Germany, Great Britain, Italy, Japan, and the United States.

Egypt has a large trade deficit — it has to import more products than it exports. Products that must be imported include flour, meat, wheat, food products, chemicals, iron, machinery and automotive vehicles, paper products, and steel.

The principle action being taken to reform the economy is called privatization — the government is transferring control of many aspects of the economy to the private business sector.

SUEZ CANAL

The Suez Canal is an important source of income for Egypt. Ships from all over the world pass through the canal instead of taking the long route around the tip of Africa.

(*A Closer Look, page 64*)

Left: **A Cairo business meeting. Privatization of businesses means that the private sector, rather than the government, has control.**

TOURISTS ARE BIG BUSINESS

Tourism is an important part of Egypt's economy. Most tourists come to visit its ancient wonders, such as the Great Pyramids, the Sphinx, and the temples.

(*A Closer Look, page 70*)

Most Egyptians are quite poor. The average per capita (per person) income in Egypt was about $1,100 per year in 1997. There is a small class of very wealthy Egyptians and a moderate sized middle class. The large group of very poor, peasant farmers are called *fellahin* (FELL-ah-heen). Agriculture is the largest employer in the economy (about 40 percent) and is almost entirely privately owned farms. About one-third of Egyptians work in government jobs, public sector enterprises, and the armed forces. Another 20 percent work in privately owned service and manufacturing enterprises. Unemployment rates are 8 to 11 percent.

Egypt's traditional capitalist economy shifted to a socialist, government-run economy during the time of President Nasser. A government-run economy is a centrally planned economy, meaning that the government owns or controls most, or all, modes of production and makes all major economic decisions.

Egyptian leaders believe it is not a good idea to change the economy too fast. As a result, Egypt has adopted a policy of economic reform that is designed to bring Egypt away from a planned economy but also to consider what Egyptian leaders believe are important social and political factors associated with changing the economy. Their goal is sustainable economic growth, which means developing an economy that will continue to grow in the future.

Below: Egypt's most economically important mineral resource is oil. Egypt has approximately six billion barrels of proven oil reserves, and exploration teams are discovering more sources each year. Egypt also has natural gas reserves, but these are currently not exploited as extensively as oil.

People and Lifestyle

About 99 percent of Egyptians trace their heritage to Egyptian, Nubian (NOO-bi-an), Bedouin (BED-oo-in), and Arabian ancestors. Most share a common cultural heritage, language (Arabic), and religion (Islam). The remaining one percent traces its heritage to Greece, Italy, Syria, or Lebanon.

People are not categorized into ethnic groups nor discriminated against because of their skin color. Most Egyptians do not think of themselves as Arab or Nubian. They simply consider themselves Egyptian.

Even though almost all Egyptians are from the same ethnic group, social class is often an important factor in determining a person's position in life. Social class is not determined by income but by birth or some combination of history, culture, lifestyle, education, and religion.

Approximately 84 percent of all Egyptians are Muslims; the rest are mostly Coptic Christians.

FELLAHIN VILLAGERS

Fellah means farmer in Arabic, and the people who live in the country and farm the land are called *fellahin*.
(A Closer Look, page 50)

Left: Fellahin children on their way to market. Over half of all Egyptians live in rural villages and towns along the Nile, sea coasts, and at the oases. A large majority of rural inhabitants are the fellahin, or peasant farmers.

20

Left: Most of Egypt's Bedouins live in the Sinai Peninsula. Sinai Bedouins belong to one of twelve tribes.

A large group distinguished within Egyptian society is the Nubians. Ancient Nubia, called Kush by the pharaohs and Ethiopia by the ancient Greeks, was located between Aswan and Khartoum in Sudan. Nubians fished, farmed, and transported goods up and down the Nile. They persisted in these traditional pursuits until the 1960s, when the Aswan High Dam was built. Because their land along the Nile from Aswan to the Sudanese border would be flooded, the people had to relocate, and their insular way of life began to change.

Another age-old, culturally distinct group of Egyptians is the Bedouins. They are probably the most distinct, although small, group of Arabic-speaking, Muslim Egyptians. Bedouins are traditionally pastoral nomads, which means their lifestyle is based on moving constantly with their sheep and camel herds in search of food for the animals. They also fish and hunt quail. Some Bedouins now live in settled villages along the Mediterranean coast and at oases. They have orchards of date palm trees, peaches, and other fruits. Others continue to follow a nomadic lifestyle. They maintain their cultural distinction through their lifestyle, traditional customs, and dress.

TAMING THE RIVER

The lives of both Bedouins and Nubians were dramatically affected by the building of the Aswan High Dam on the Nile River. Today, Bedouins are less nomadic, and Nubians are assimilated into Egyptian society.

(A Closer Look, page 68)

21

Family Life

For most Egyptians, life revolves around family relationships. Marriage and the birth of children mark the most important events in any Egyptian's life. Legally, a girl may not marry before age sixteen or a boy before age eighteen. Among many middle and upper class Egyptians, marriage may be somewhat later. Girls and boys do not "date" in Egypt as they do in the West. The only exception to this general rule is among some of Egypt's elite, who are very Westernized in their dress and behavior.

It is not proper for a boy and girl to be alone together. From about the age of eight or ten, boys and girls are kept very separate. Even at home, boys work and play with their brothers and fathers, while girls tend to be with their sisters and mothers, doing household work.

Except in school or a similar environment, boys and girls are not supposed to talk with each other. A girl seen talking with a boy or a man who is not in her family could ruin her honor and that of her family. She would be punished by her family, lose face among her friends, and probably would not get a "good" husband.

Above: Egyptians enjoy simple family outings, but even among children, the girls and boys tend to remain in separate groups.

JOYFUL OCCASIONS

Weddings are big events in Egypt. Often the entire village will attend, and in the cities, the wedding receptions are often held at grand hotels.

(A Closer Look, page 58)

Many marriages, although certainly not all, are arranged by an agreement between families. Sometimes the boy and girl know each other; sometimes they do not. Among the Bedouin and fellahin, marriages may be arranged when the child is very young.

Marriage is a two-step process. Step one involves negotiation and signing a marriage contract. Step two, which may occur immediately or six months to a year later, is the actual announcement that the couple will live as husband and wife. Celebrations occur at each stage of the marriage, especially when the wife gives birth. Children are considered gifts from God, and the larger the family, the more blessed it is.

As a general rule of thumb, men are responsible for working in some activity that provides money for the family's sustenance, whereas women are responsible for household and child-rearing activities. Although these are broad statements, they tend to hold true throughout Egyptian society, regardless of the family's status or income. Most Egyptians view the distinction between men's and women's roles as complimentary — in other words, both are necessary and respected for contributing to family needs.

Below: **Families visit graves on** *Eid el-Adha* **to commemorate the sacrifice of Abraham. When someone dies, an** *Imam* **(EE-mahm) recites prayers to Allah, and mourners say silent prayers. Then the Qur'an is read, and food is given to the poor.**

Education

Part of Egyptian children's education is their formal schooling or training. Another part is the informal or non-classroom training boys and girls need to learn the appropriate roles they will play later as adults in society. Statistics estimate that 51.4 percent of the Egyptian population over age fifteen is literate. The number is much higher for men than it is for women. The Egyptian government has placed a high priority on raising the literacy rate and is taking many steps to ensure that more Egyptians are prepared to meet the next century.

Formal schooling, highly valued for both boys and girls among the middle and upper classes, begins at about five years of age. Although primary school (for children aged six to twelve years) is compulsory, many families do not send all their children to school. Most poor people feel that their children can better learn what they need in life by working on the farm or in family businesses. University education is tuition-free for students who pass the qualifying exams, but many face pressure to work instead, because their families are dependent on their income.

Below: **Carpet weaving is an acceptable trade for girls to learn. Their small, delicate fingers are ideally suited for the thousands of tiny knots that make up a carpet.**

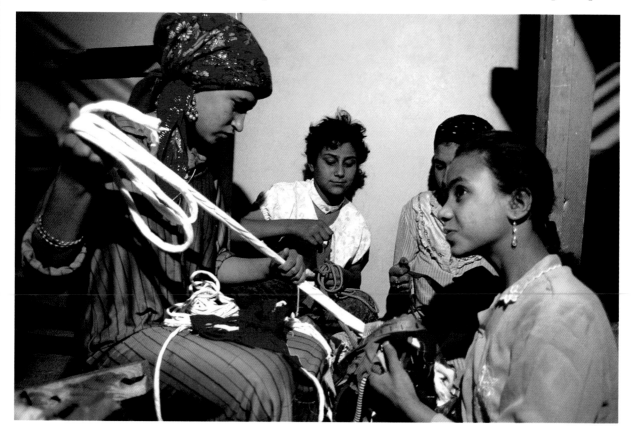

Left: The Arabic alphabet has twenty-eight letters and fourteen symbols that function as short vowels and pronunciation markers. The letters have different forms depending on where they are in a word.

After completing primary school, students may enter preparatory school, which lasts three years. Then students must take an exam to determine whether they may go on to a general school or a specialized secondary school. General schools prepare students for a university education in the sciences or humanities. Specialized secondary schools prepare them for trade or technical professions. To acquire a secondary school certificate, students must pass a national qualifying exam. Depending on a student's ranking nationally, he or she may be eligible to attend a university. What a student is allowed to study is also determined by his or her ranking on the exam.

From an early age, daily activities tend to be different for boys and girls. Among farming families, children usually help in the daily work done by their parents. For instance, boys work in the fields or fish with their fathers and brothers. Girls take care of children, wash dishes and clothes, and learn to sew, cook, and bargain. Families who are in business give their sons opportunities to learn about the business. Except for carpet weaving and a few other crafts, girls typically are not seen in public places of business.

TEA BOYS

Young boys are often seen at their father's place of business, where they learn what they will need to know as adults. For example, a boy may be a "tea boy" at his father's shop. This means he is responsible for serving tea or cold drinks to guests in the shop. Egyptians like to make guests feel welcome, whether in the home or at work.

Left: The Mosque of Muhammad 'Ali is in the Citadel, a huge medieval fortress. The center dome, half domes, and tall minarets are impressive monuments to Muhammad 'Ali, ruler of Egypt in the early nineteenth century.

Religion

About 84 percent of all Egyptians are Muslims, people who practice the religion called Islam. Islam is the official religion of Egypt. Before the arrival of Islam into Egypt in the seventh century, most Egyptians were Christian. Approximately 15 percent of Egyptians today are Christian.

Muslims

The word *Islam* means "having peace with God" or "submission to God." *Allah* is the Arabic word for God. The Muslim holy book is called the Qur'an (KOUR-aan), or Koran. Friday is the holy day of the week. Islam is a complete way of life that combines religion and culture with manners and morals. By living according to the word of Allah as told to the Prophet Muhammad, Muslims believe that they will find peace with their faith and with those around them.

Most Egyptians are Sunni Muslims, one of the two major religious divisions in Islam. The country is not a strict Muslim state. Religious courts are banned, and children are educated by the state rather than the mosque.

ANCIENT GODS AND GODDESSES

The ancient Egyptians believed in many gods and goddesses who represented the powers of nature, magic, and ritual. The pharaohs themselves were considered gods. They also believed in life after death and spent much time and expense on preparing elaborate tombs for the afterlife.

Coptic Christians

Most Egyptian Christians belong to the Coptic Christian Church. The word *Copt* is derived from the Greek word meaning "Egyptian." Egypt became Christian very early, probably in the time of the Apostles. St. Mark, the author of the second Gospel, is regarded as the founder of the Christian Coptic Church. According to legend, he came to Egypt sometime after Jesus' death and died in Alexandria. Before this time, Egyptians were polytheists. They worshiped many gods and goddesses who represented different forms of nature, life, and death.

Christianity grew, although in the second century believers were persecuted for their faith. Later, as a province of the Roman Empire, Egypt officially became a Christian country, following the decree of Emperor Constantine in A.D. 312. It remained Christian until the Arab conquest of Egypt in the 640s.

The Copts have always produced an educated elite in Egypt. Many successful business people are Copts. The most famous Copt today is the former United Nations Secretary General, Boutros Boutros-Ghali.

Below: A Christian nun takes a walk with some local schoolchildren. The Copts have established their own schools, but these are open to Muslims as well.

Language and Literature

Arabic has been the official language of Egypt for thirteen centuries. Before the Arab invasion in the seventh century A.D., Coptic was the official language. Today, the Coptic language is only used in the Coptic Church, and Arabic is the language of Copts and Muslims alike.

Spoken Arabic has developed into various local dialects, several of which are spoken in Egypt. However, Egyptian Colloquial Arabic is understood by most Arabic speakers because Egypt has been a leader in television and film, which exposes the Arabic-speaking world to this form of the language. Written or classical Arabic is the language of the Qur'an and is used in most textbooks for learning written Arabic.

Arabic script is written from right to left. Written Arabic is truly an art form. Some styles are written in very flowery *calligraphy*, which in Arabic means "the art of handwriting." Egyptians both speak and write with a flowery eloquence, unlike English verbal or written patterns. Among Arabic speakers, words possess power. Conversations also contain frequent

Below: **Ancient Egyptians wrote in hieroglyphics, a kind of picture script, on paper made from the papyrus plant. They also carved hieroglyphic symbols on temple walls and rocks.**

Left: **Najib Mahfouz won the Nobel Prize for Literature in 1988 for the Cairo Trilogy —** *Palace Walk, Palace of Desire,* **and** *Sugar Street.* **He uses the dialect and slang of ordinary people to make his characters real, and his works provide insightful perspectives on Egyptian life.**

blessings. These blessings serve the purpose of showing that the speaker wants things to go well.

Egyptian novels, poetry, and plays have deep traditional roots in Islamic history. Many write about Western influence on Egypt, as in Tawfig al-Hakim's novel, *The Bird from the East.* Others write romantically about the Egyptian countryside, as in Muhammad Husayn Haykal's *Zaynab.* Haykal was one of the earliest modern Arabic writers, with his first novel written in 1914. Currently, the most famous writer in Egypt is Najib Mahfouz, whose novels have been translated into many languages. He won the Nobel Prize for Literature in 1988. Other famous Egyptian writers include Taha Husayn, Mahmud Taymur, and Abbas al-Aqqad.

The first Arabic-language plays were performed in 1870, and, since then, playwrights, such as Tawfig al-Hakim and Mahmud Taymur, have written about the cultural and social history of the country, as well as the changes that have affected modern Egypt.

WONDERFUL EXPRESSIONS

The Egyptian language is flowery, colorful, and full of expression. The one word that perhaps best describes the character of the people is the commonly used term *maalesh* (MAH-lesh). It means "it doesn't matter," "too bad," or "take it easy," and is used in many situations.

Arts

Art abounds in Egypt, ranging from ancient sculptures and paintings to modern advertising sign boards decorated in psychedelic colors. Art played a vital role in ancient Egyptian culture. It was not art "for art's sake," but served to translate religious experiences into a visual form. Ancient Egyptians used several forms of art: sculpture, relief, and painting.

Ancient Egyptian artists depicted people and objects by using their most characteristic aspects. All figures were shown in an idealized, perfect form. Men were young and handsome; women were slim and beautiful. Age, deformity, and illness were deliberately excluded. Figures (whether in sculpture, painting, or relief) were posed standing, sitting, or kneeling rather than in action. Even when action scenes were depicted, such as a person hunting or spearing a fish, the figures were shown with a perfectly balanced body in the midst of action, giving the observer the impression of controlled power.

SUZANNE MUBARAK AND EDUCATION

The Suzanne Mubarak Museum for Children, just outside Cairo, was built especially for children to explore and learn.
(A Closer Look, page 66)

Left: **The temple of Ramses II carved into rock at Abu Simbel, near Aswan. Ramses was the longest reigning pharaoh and had many years to perfect his monuments.**

The most distinctive characteristic of ancient Egyptian paintings and reliefs is the use of two-dimensional representations. People and objects are flat, depicting a concept rather than an image. Human representations were a composite of parts, each of which was designed to show the typical aspect of that part of the body. For example, the head was shown in profile, but with a full-view eye, eyebrow, and half mouth.

Stories in Paintings

Ancient paintings and reliefs tell a story. Scenes depicted on the walls of tombs or temples are of two basic types: formal scenes and daily life activities. Formal scenes show the world of the gods and the dead. In temples, these scenes illustrate the kings performing rituals for the gods as well as acts by the gods toward the king. In tombs, the subject matter centers around daily activities.

Subordinates were not shown in an idealized form or in a formal posture, but could be shown dancing, fighting, or farming. In both types of scenes, the bigger the figure, the more important he or she was. The king and gods were usually shown in equal size, to indicate the godliness of the king.

Above: The golden shrine in the burial chamber of King Tutankhamun. Since "King Tut" was only a boy when he died, many archaeologists thought his tomb would contain little of interest. English Egyptologist Howard Carter proved them wrong when he opened the tomb.

Left: **Unlike previous Egyptian pharaohs, who had worshiped an array of gods, Pharaoh Akhenaten and his wife, Nefertiti, worshiped one true God called Aten. Akhenaten's favorite works of art featured himself and Nefertiti in domestic scenes or in the presence of Aten, depicted as a golden orb radiating beams of light toward the royal couple. Amarna Art, as this style is called, abandoned more stylized depictions of the pharaoh in favor of a more realistic portrayal of royal domestic life.**

Sculpture and Relief

Sculpture in the round developed early in Egypt. Artists used limestone, diorite, and alabaster. Royal figures from the time of the pharaohs are sculpted in the round, either alone or paired with their wives. They are usually shown walking, seated, or kneeling.

Reliefs were architectural in inspiration. Wall sculpture was usually done in bas-relief, where the background was cut away. Several forms of sunken relief, where the figures were carved into the stone, were also used. Sunken relief was much faster and cheaper to make and was used particularly for inscriptions.

Egypt is the site of two of the Seven Wonders of the Ancient World: the Pharos Lighthouse at Alexandria and the Great Pyramids at Giza. The lighthouse is gone, but the three Great Pyramids at Giza, near Cairo, are an architectural wonder whose precise method of construction is still debated by scholars today. Khufu's pyramid, the largest of the three, is 450 feet (137 m) high. It is made up of at least 2,300,000 stone blocks, each weighing an average of 2.5 tons.

Crafts

Egypt has a long tradition of crafts and folk art. The Bedouins, for example, have beautiful embroidery and jewelry. Traditional craft materials are brass, copper, ivory, silver, and gold. Copper and brass are used to make trays, mirror frames, vases, and coffee pots. They are carefully worked by hand and may also have inlays for added decoration. Much of today's Egyptian art, especially souvenirs for tourists, involves making copies of ancient works. Calligraphy, an invention of Islamic writing, adds beauty and form to contemporary art works. Some artisans still make clay pottery, as well as alabaster vases and decorative objects.

Above: **Famous composer George Kazazian plays the lute.**

Left: **A young boy engraves designs on a brass plate.**

33

Leisure and Festivals

Egyptians have different priorities for leisure than Westerners do. The Western concept of leisure is usually associated with "doing" something or "going" somewhere, such as bowling, movies, or sports. As a general rule, the most important leisure activity in Egypt is visiting with friends or family. Most city quarters contain households connected by kinship or close personal ties to one another. This connection results in close cooperation among households and provides an essential support network for women. Women develop a close cluster of friends and relatives, and daily visits are common.

Women tend to do most of their socializing in private places, such as in the home. If they live in the city, women may go to the park with their children and other women. If they live near the coast, they may take a family outing at the beach. In small rural villages, women may gather in groups to chat around the well or at the river when they are washing dishes.

Below: **Family outings at the beach are a popular way to celebrate a holiday.**

Left: **The most important leisure activity in Egypt is enjoying family and friends. Here, the children are having a donkey ride.**

Women are responsible for the informal education and discipline of young children, especially in terms of teaching cultural and religious traditions. Folk tales are one way they teach children values and traditions. Many folk tales concern ethical dilemmas between right and wrong or good and bad, or the value of a good marriage. A common theme is how the wise or smart person is able to "trick" an unscrupulous person. In these tales, the "good, smart" person invariably wins out over the "bad, greedy" person.

Most Egyptian women rarely leave the house without their children and a family male to accompany them, although after arriving at their destination, men and women almost always socialize separately. When visiting the homes of friends or family, men most often talk with men in one room while women talk with women in another. Children may socialize with other children, their parents, or other relatives.

Men have more visible social lives than women. A favorite pastime for men is gathering in the evening at a local café to play dominoes or other board games.

Walking through the city to shop or enjoying a stroll along the Nile are favorite activities of married couples. The streets of Cairo are alive at night with couples and their children shopping and enjoying the sights, smells, and tastes from the myriad of street vendors and small cafés.

Sports

Soccer (called football) is Egypt's principal sporting interest. Egypt also has basketball, polo, swimming, water polo, squash, volleyball, and handball teams. None of these, however, inspires the interest and attention given to soccer. Thousands of cheering fans attend soccer games or watch matches on television. The two main stadiums are the Cairo National Stadium and the Military Academy Stadium.

Because sports in Egypt are typically limited to private sports clubs rather than being associated with school events, participation in organized sporting events is generally limited to those who can afford membership in the exclusive clubs. The Military Officers Sports Club, for example, is an important club that encourages sporting events among men attending the Egyptian Military Academy.

Two teams top Egypt's soccer club agenda: the al-Ahly Club and the Zamalek Club. *Al-Ahly* means "national." The club is located in Cairo, and its colors are red and white. Al-Ahly has been league champion twenty-six times and cup winner thirty-one times, a

URBAN JUNGLE

Dodging traffic in the busy, urban rush hour in Cairo is a sport in itself. There are few traffic lights and even fewer sidewalks, and sometimes there are as many as eight lanes of traffic for a pedestrian to cross.

(A Closer Look, page 72)

Below: Soccer games around the pyramids. Races and horseback riding around these monuments are other popular sports.

Left: **Lawn bowling at a private club in Cairo. Many sports and leisure activities are enjoyed only by the wealthy, who can afford to belong to exclusive clubs like this one.**

record in Egypt. The club also won the African Cup Winners Cup four times — 1984, 1985, 1986, and 1993. One of their best known players was el-Kateeb, who was the African footballer of 1983.

The Zamalek Club is also located in Cairo. Its uniform jerseys are white with two red stripes, and the shorts are white. The Zamalek Club was league champion eight times and cup winner eighteen times. One of the club's most well known players is Emmanuel Amunike, who was the African footballer for 1994.

In May 1996, Egypt hosted the al Ahram International Squash Tournament, in front of the Giza pyramids. This tournament had many competitions, from track events to horse racing. Egypt's leading squash star, Ahmed Barada, placed second in this tournament, and the team maintained a fourteenth ranking in international tournaments. Egypt's young athletes also rank highly. Ahmad Faizy won first place in the 1995 Junior Squash World Championship.

Egypt sent several athletes, including women, to the Atlanta Olympics held in 1996. Among these Olympians were Rania Elwany (African women's swimming champion), Heba Rashid (Egypt's women's judo star), and Egypt's high-ranking handball team — 1993 Junior World Champions.

WRESTLING AND WEIGHT LIFTING

Wrestling and weight lifting were the first sports at which Egypt excelled internationally. Weight lifter Nasser el Sayed won Egypt's first gold medal in the 1928 Olympics. Also, the Olympic swim team is one of the best in Africa, and their squash teams are world class.

Major Holidays and Festivals

Friday is Egypt's weekend holiday. People in government offices work from Saturday through Thursday. In the private sector, people often work only five days per week, from Sunday through Thursday if they are Muslim, and from Monday through Friday if they are Christian.

All Muslims celebrate three major festivals: *Moulid el-Nabi* (MOO-led el-NAH-bi), *Eid el-Adha* (EYE-eed el-AD-hah), and *Eid el-Fitr* (EYE-eed el-FIT-er).

Moulid el-Nabi celebrates the birth of Prophet Muhammad and begins on the eve of the eleventh day of the third month in the Islamic calendar. People decorate their homes and put up tents in open areas next to their homes, where male guests and relatives take their holiday meals and participate in the prescribed religious rituals.

On any of the evenings prior to the festival day, recitation and chants praising Allah can be heard over microphones in the neighborhood. Many families celebrate the holiday by eating a big meal at home, although those who can afford it may take their family to one of the big mosques in Cairo to celebrate. During the festivities, merchants sell a brightly colored candy doll that is an Egyptian symbol for the Prophet's birthday.

MOULID

A *moulid* (MOO-led) celebrates the birth of a saint or a prophet. Moulids are held near the tombs of saints, but the atmosphere is not solemn. People dance and clap and sing. There are children's rides, sideshows, and food stands. Moulids usually last about a week, and thousands come to receive a blessing from the saint and to have fun.

Below: Sufis belong to a mystical order of Muslims that emphasizes trances through dancing, as a direct personal experience with God.

Eid el-Adha (the big feast) lasts three days and is celebrated after the annual pilgrimage to Mecca in Saudi Arabia. It opens with prayers by men at the local mosque, after which many people go to the cemetery in memory of the dead. Eid el-Adha is the festival of sacrifices, and many people buy a sheep or cow to slaughter after morning prayers on the first day. The sheep-slaying ritual commemorates the Qur'anic story of Abraham's willingness to sacrifice his eldest son, Ishmael; when God saw Abraham's faith, He commanded that a sheep be slaughtered instead.

Observation of the holy month of *Ramadan* (RA-ma-DAAN), the ninth month in the Islamic calendar, is one of the most important events in any year. It is the month during which the Prophet Muhammad received Allah's revelations. Ramadan is the month of fasting. People fast throughout the day and break their fast only at sunset. Eid el-Fitr (the little feast) is celebrated at the end of Ramadan.

Sham el-Nessim (Scent of Spring) is a festival that has its roots in the time of the pharaohs. This traditional festival takes place on Easter Monday. In ancient days, families took leisurely cruises down the Nile on flower-decorated *feluccas* (feh-LUKE-kahs), or traditional sailboats. Now, people celebrate Sham el-Nessim by having picnics in gardens and parks along the Nile.

Above: **Schoolchildren practice for a musical they will perform during Ramadan.**

CHRISTIANS IN EGYPT

Coptic Christians, a minority, celebrate Christmas on January 7. After a midnight service, children receive new clothes and gifts. Sunday is the Coptic religious day. It is a working day in Egypt, but Copts may take time off to attend church.
(*A Closer Look, page 44*)

Food

Western fast-food restaurants are rapidly invading the major cities in Egypt. Cairo is now home to hamburger, pizza, and fried chicken fast-food restaurants. These specialty restaurants, frequented by foreigners and Westernized Egyptians, do not represent typical Egyptian food. Local restaurants, cafés, and street vendors serve more traditional foods, and some serve sophisticated recipes copied and adapted from Western cuisine. Except for a few distinctly Egyptian dishes, the Egyptian diet tends to combine Turkish, Greek, Palestinian, Lebanese, and Syrian foods and styles of cooking, modified to suit Egyptian tastes.

Bread, *foul* (FOOL), and *ta'miya* (ta-MEE-ya) make up the staples in a typical Egyptian diet. Egyptian bread is similar to pita bread. It is flat, unleavened, and, when it is baked in a hot oven or over coals, puffs up to make an air pocket inside two outer shells. Foul is boiled fava beans. Ta'miya, which is also called *felafel* (fey-LAH-fal), is fried balls of chickpeas and wheat.

FASTING

Muslim Egyptians do not eat in the daytime during the holy month of Ramadan. They break their fast at sunset.
(A Closer Look, page 48)

Below: **Ovens such as these are used to bake flat, pita-like bread. You can make a pocket in the bread and stuff it with all sorts of ingredients or eat it with tasty dips.**

Lunch is served sometime between 2:00 and 5:00 p.m. Dinner, in the evening, consists of leftovers from lunch or is a simple supper of bread, cold meat, pickles, and eggs. Starches, mainly rice and bread, form the mainstays of the Egyptian lunch and dinner. These are usually served with vegetables cooked with meat, chicken, or fish. Sheep and goat meat is more common than beef. Lunch and dinner may be accompanied by puddings or sweet cakes. Beverages served with all meals may be hot or cold. All are non-alcoholic.

Egyptians tend to take their larger meal in mid-afternoon rather than at night. However, when guests are present for the evening meal, the meal can be quite substantial.

Food is an important part of the Egyptian expression of hospitality and generosity. It is very important for Egyptians of all economic levels to present themselves well when visitors come over and to make their guests feel welcome. Even if the family cannot afford it, they will often offer an extravagant meal to visitors. The principle rule for being a good host is to provide plenty of food. The principle rule for being a good guest is to eat a lot!

BARBECUES

Kofta and kebab are two popular dishes. Kebab is meat or chicken pieces, and kofta is ground beef or lamb. Both are grilled on skewers over a fire, usually with tomatoes and onions.

A CLOSER LOOK
AT EGYPT

This section takes a closer look at Egypt today. The awesome pyramids and temples of its ancient civilization are of little relevance to the daily lives of Egyptians today, except for those who work in the tourism business. Tourism is a big business, however, and provides many jobs — guides, drivers, sellers and makers of handicrafts, hotel workers, and entertainers.

Egypt's biggest accomplishments in recent history are the building of the Aswan High Dam and peace with Israel. The relations between Egypt and other countries in the Middle East and North America are good, but growth and change have not necessarily meant prosperity. Egypt is struggling to deal with its huge population and rampant poverty.

Most Egyptians lead simple lives, unaffected by the glamour of tourism. They are farmers or government workers living in villages or city apartments and doing many of the same things families do everywhere within the confines of their government, their religion, and their values.

Opposite: **About half the children of Egypt are literate by the age of fifteen. Boys tend to be better educated than girls, who tend to leave school at a younger age to take on the traditional roles of wife and mother.**

Below: **Children play in the park, a popular spot for families to celebrate holidays and talk with friends.**

Christians in Egypt

As a province of the Christian Roman Empire, Egypt officially became a Christian country in A.D. 312. The origins, however, of Christianity in Egypt go back to the earliest days in the history of the religion. St. Mark is said to have arrived in Egypt around forty or fifty years after the death of Jesus. He was killed near Alexandria during an Easter celebration in A.D. 68, when celebrants of the ancient polytheistic religion turned on the Christians.

The new religion grew steadily throughout the first 200 years, then Christians began to be persecuted for their beliefs. In 284, more than three hundred churches were closed, literature was destroyed, officials dismissed, and Christians were forbidden to meet. By the early fourth century, however, the persecution had ceased, and the power of the Coptic community grew rapidly. The head of the Christian Church became one of the most influential figures in Egypt.

After the arrival of Islam in the seventh century, Christianity began to die out and today, Copts and other Christians are a minority in Egypt.

Below: **The Monastery of St. Anthony was built in the barren cliffs of the Eastern Desert in the fourth century by disciples of St. Anthony who gave up their worldly possessions to devote their lives to God.**

Left: **A Coptic priest at prayer. Coptic Christians trace their faith back to the earliest development of Christianity in the first century. Unlike other Christians, Copts believe that a god cannot be both human and divine. Other branches of Christianity believe that Jesus was both human and divine.**

The Holy Family in Egypt

The Bible states that when Jesus Christ was born, God appeared to Joseph and said, "Arise, and take the young child and his mother, and flee into Egypt, and be thou there until I bring the word." (Matt. 2:13). These words from the Christian Bible form the basis of the story of the holy family in Egypt. They left Israel for Egypt to escape persecution by King Herod of Jerusalem and remained there until Herod's death.

Although the holy family's exact route is not recorded, if they left Bethlehem, Israel, and took the traditional caravan route, they would have passed through Gaza, Israel, then through the frontier town of Rafah (now on the border in Egypt), and on into Egypt. Once in Egypt, the family stopped at the village of Matariyah, now a suburb of Cairo, where the Garden of Balsam (Balm) developed. The holy family then went to where the Church of the Blessed Virgin now stands in a northeastern district of old Cairo. Continuing southward, the family passed the Fortress of Babylon and went as far as Asyut before beginning their journey back north through Egypt.

Clothes and Veils

Egyptians wear a wide range of clothing styles. Around universities, people wear Western-style clothing, for the most part, but often dress a little more formally than many students in Western countries. Businessmen and women generally dress in Western-style business clothes. Men wear suits with ties, while women wear dresses or suits. Well-to-do Egyptian women wear the latest European fashions; however, they usually choose long-sleeved garments and fairly long skirts. Egyptians are very conservative in their dress, and wearing revealing clothes in public is not considered appropriate. So, for example, women do not wear mini skirts.

Women usually accessorize their dresses with gold or silver jewelry but almost never wear costume jewelry. Except in the highest fashion areas and around universities, Egyptian women do not usually wear long pants or slacks, and blue jeans are mostly worn only by male students.

The most visible clothing seen in Egypt is the traditional *galabea* (GAHL-ah-BAY-yah), an ankle-length, loose garment worn by men and women. Men usually wear white, beige, gray, or light blue galabeas. Women tend to like more color and some embroidery, or black if they are more traditional.

Above: **Fashion shows in Cairo and Alexandria feature the latest Western styles.**

Below: **Schoolchildren typically wear a mix of Egyptian and Western clothing, such as jeans and sports shoes with loose shirts.**

Left: **Many Egyptians wear the traditional galabea, a long, loose shirt. It is comfortable in the heat and provides protection from the sun. Galabeas can be simple like these or embroidered with lovely designs in bright colors. In summer, people wear light cotton galabeas, and in winter, heavier ones.**

Scarves and Veils

Many women in Egypt wear a large scarf fitted snugly around the face and under the chin. They wear scarves because unobtrusive clothing and being covered up is part of the conservative society in Egypt. The scarves, however, may be quite beautiful and trimmed with beads.

Only in very conservative families in Egypt do women wear face veils. Many scholars believe that veiling is a very old tradition. At the time of Prophet Muhammad, only wealthy or influential women used the veil. When the Prophet and his followers fled in A.D. 622 from Mecca to Medina, in Saudi Arabia, some of his followers suggested that his women followers should wear the veil so believers could be distinguished from others. After that, wearing a veil became a visible symbol of women who believed in Islam. Wearing a cloak or over-garment also signaled to all who saw them that these women were special. Later, the act of veiling was legitimized in the Qur'an.

Fasting

Ramadan is the ninth month of the Islamic calendar. It was during this month that the Angel Gabriel is said to have revealed the word of God (Allah) to the Prophet Muhammad. Since the Islamic calendar is a lunar calendar, the month of Ramadan begins when the new crescent moon is seen. Even though modern equipment can be used to calculate the beginning of Ramadan, Muslims prefer to use the human eye. If the new moon is seen on the twenty-ninth day of *Shaaban* (SHA-AB-an, the eighth month), then Ramadan starts the next day. If not, then Ramadan will start the day after.

The holy month of Ramadan is a month of fasting for Muslims. The idea of fasting existed in most ancient religions and remains important in the three major monotheistic religions (religions believing in one God). Jews fast for Yom Kippur, Christians for Lent, and Muslims for Ramadan. Among Muslims, fasting starts at the first light of day and ends at sunset.

Below: **Praying is one of the most important beliefs in Islam. Five times every day, the *muezzin* (MUH-a-zin) makes the call to prayer throughout the cities and villages. Whatever they are doing, all Muslims stop to pray.**

Evening meals to break the fast, called *iftar* (IFF-tar), are provided by the wealthy and served outside the main mosques. The word *iftar* actually means "break the fast," and the meal is eaten at sunset. According to tradition, the Prophet Muhammad broke the fast with a few dates soaked in milk. Afterward, he performed his prayers and had a main meal. Today, iftar starts with a sweet juice, such as apricot juice, or dried dates soaked in water with sugar. After the juice, soup is served, followed by meat dishes, rice, and salad. Families also often eat a lot of sweets during the evenings.

Sahour (sa-HOO-ur) is the last meal of the day before the fast starts at dawn. An Egyptian sahour usually includes *foul (FOOL)* beans or lentils, yogurt, cheese, vegetables or salad, bread, and something sweet. Many rules regulate Ramadan, but, basically, all adults are obligated to fast between dawn and dusk during the month. Children are not required to fast until they reach a certain age, but are encouraged to do so as soon as they are able.

Eid al-Fitr celebrates the end of Ramadan and is the most important family holiday in Egypt. Everyone returns home to celebrate with relatives.

Above: **Women prepare a Ramadan iftar meal. The holy month of Ramadan is a very important part of Islam. After people break their fast in the evening, they will talk and sing with friends, go together to the mosque to pray, and listen to Qur'an readings. Even shops stay open late.**

Fellahin Villagers

The term *fellahin* originates from the Arabic word *fellah*, meaning farmer. Originally, the term was used simply to distinguish between the nomadic Bedouins and the settled farmers. Today, the term refers to small-scale farmers whose lifestyle has only recently begun to change with mechanized cultivation and government-sponsored social programs. More fellahin have gained ownership of land since the Egyptian revolution, but many still work for or rent land to cultivate from large landholders.

More than half of the population of Egypt are farmers who live in rural areas. Large families are common, although the government is seeking to educate parents on the advantages of smaller families. The fellahin typically live in one of the many small villages along the Nile banks and the delta.

Below: **Peasant farmers work in rich soil near the Nile. Behind them is the Temple of Kom Ombo.**

Above: **Village women wash clothes and dishes in a nearby irrigation canal. Water for use in cooking and other household needs is carried home in large plastic jugs.**

Frequently, a fellahin village is made up of a group of people who are related. Often, all the families are descendants of one couple who started the village about three or four generations earlier. Most of the crops grown are used for subsistence or are traded for food items not grown in the village or for other household necessities. The men and boys in the village also fish and sell their produce in nearby towns or in the city of Cairo. Sometimes a village may share one tractor, but most farm work is done by hand.

A village often has several houses, all constructed of mud brick. Houses have flat roofs, with small staircases leading to the top. Children sleep on the roofs during the hot summer months. Windows are open spaces in the walls for ventilation but do not have glass or screens over the openings. Doors are the same. Each house has a special room for guests. This room usually has a carpet and a low table. Guests sit around the table on which food is served when they visit.

The kitchen is an unenclosed area outside the house. It has an open-hearth for cooking and no modern appliances. Villagers use dried cow dung for cooking fuel. Many villages do not have modern sewage systems. The Nile River and irrigation canals are used instead for washing and toilet facilities.

Fights with Neighbors

The Six-Day War

The establishment of Israel in 1948 resulted in immediate clashes with Arab countries and the flight of thousands of Palestinians from their homeland (because it had been taken over by Israel) into surrounding Arab countries. Egypt and Israel fought in 1948 and 1956. Tensions continued to exist, and hostilities increased in the 1960s.

On the morning of June 5, 1967, Israel launched a full-scale attack against Egypt and Jordan. By June 11, Arab defeat was complete. Israel had expanded its borders to include all of historic Palestine (including Jerusalem), the West Bank, the Gaza Strip, part of the Sinai, and the Golan Heights in Syria. These areas have since been termed the "occupied territories."

Egypt's losses in the war with Israel were tremendous: 11,500 military personnel were killed; 5,000 were captured; and 80 percent of their military equipment was destroyed. The Sinai was under Israel's control, and the Suez Canal was blocked and closed to shipping.

Below: **Egyptian President Anwar al-Sadat** *(front, right)* **and Palestinian Authority leader Yasser Arafat** *(front, left).*

The October War

The 1967 war with Israel was a humiliating defeat for Egypt. It resulted in a stalemate — no peace, no war. Egypt's economy was drained as it tried to rebuild its military afterward. By 1972, President Anwar al-Sadat felt considerable pressure from within Egypt to go to war against Israel as the only way to regain lost territories and to force Israel to the bargaining table.

The October War was launched on October 6, 1973, when Egypt executed a successful surprise attack across the Suez Canal. At the same time, the Syrians carried out an attack from the north. United Nations Emergency Forces arrived to enforce a cease-fire, in time to avoid a collision between the United States, which supported Israel, and the Soviet Union, which supported Egypt.

Neither side really won, but for Egypt it was a victory because their armed forces had proven that the Israeli forces were not invincible. Sadat's prestige grew tremendously among the Egyptian people. He was able to implement the programs he wanted within Egypt, and the war led to peace negotiations with Israel.

Above: **The Sinai Peninsula was occupied by Israel from 1967 until 1979. Even afterward, Egypt did not regain full sovereignty over it, and a multinational observer force was stationed there.**

YOM KIPPUR WAR

In Israel, the 1973 war is called the Yom Kippur War because it occurred on this most important Jewish religious holiday. When attacked by Egypt, no one in Israel was at work or prepared to fight.

Gift of the Nile

Egypt, a desert country with a ribbon of water snaking its way from south to north, gets almost no rainfall. Until the 1970s, life in Egypt depended on the Nile and its annual flood. Herodotus, a Greek writer in the fifth century B.C., called Egypt "the gift of the Nile." Settlement in Egypt began because the Nile provided a predictable source of fresh water that was necessary for living in this barren, hot land. Annual flooding brought much needed water for irrigation, and each flood deposited nutrient-rich, dark soil when the waters receded. Egyptians today talk about how much better food tasted before the flooding was stopped by dams.

Beginning with the earliest civilization, people living along the Nile were very much aware of their environment. Although they were not able to make a scientific analysis of the environment, they were able to predict events by watching the movement of birds, animals, and the river. Because new soil was laid down in a belt all along the river, and because the river was a continual source of water, Egyptians were among the first people in the area to develop methods of irrigation — as early as 5,000 B.C.

Below: **The Nile River at Aswan. Aswan, in southern Egypt, is the last city before the Sudanese border. It is famous for its High Dam, which controls the waters of the Nile flowing from Upper to Lower Egypt.**

A Green Belt for Farming

Most Egyptians live along a narrow path on either side of the Nile. This "green belt" extends only for a short distance on the western and eastern sides of the river. About 40 percent of all Egyptians engage in some form of farming on this green corridor. Farming practices have changed little over the last two thousand years, and much of the work continues to be done by human labor and without much technical or mechanical equipment.

From historical times to the present day, Egypt has been divided into two regions: Upper Egypt and Lower Egypt. Upper Egypt includes the area from Cairo south to the Sudanese border; Lower Egypt, or the Nile Delta, is the area from Cairo north to the Mediterranean Sea. Lower Egypt consists of the river delta and brackish lagoons. Looking at a modern map, these terms may seem backward since north is usually at the top of the map. Egyptians, however, follow the Nile River, which flows from south to north. Therefore, it is only logical that "upper" Egypt would be "up-river," or southern Egypt.

Above: **The Nile cuts through the desert, giving life to the land on either side.**

Irrigation

Irrigation is the practice of artificially supplying water to land to sustain crop growth. Egyptians began irrigating their land nearly seven thousand years ago. Diversion dams and water-lifting machines permitted irrigation of lands lying above those normally flooded by the Nile. Modern irrigation systems are still based on these two principles.

Most of the arable land in Egypt, which is only 4 percent of the total land area, was irrigated until recently by a method called "basin irrigation." The basic principle behind basin irrigation is

capturing high water from the floods and diverting it into the fields through the use of dikes and levees interconnected by a series of canals. This process is an adaptation to the natural rhythm of the Nile, which experienced a gradual, but massive flood every year from July through October.

The flood was caused by seasonal rains in central East Africa and the Ethiopian highlands. The floodwaters carried suspended mud and silt. When farmers captured the muddy water behind their levees and dikes, a new layer of fertile top soil was deposited each year as the waters receded.

Above: **Children play in an irrigation ditch. Until recently, many peasants did not have running water in their homes. They used canals and rivers for washing clothes, bathing, and even urinating. Improved plumbing and health education are gradually changing some of these habits.**

Farmers built a series of crisscrossed dikes, 10 to 15 feet (3 to 4.5 m) high and up to 20 feet (6 m) wide. The dikes trapped water in the fields by enclosing rectangular areas of farmland to form crop basins. During the nineteenth century, these crop basins averaged 8,750 acres (3,541 hectares) each. Other lands were irrigated by hauling water to them from wells, the river, or canals.

Beginning in the nineteenth century, the country started moving toward what is termed "perennial irrigation." Perennial irrigation means the land can be watered more evenly all through the year by controlling the flooding through large dams. Perennial irrigation is based on the principle that the water stays at a low and relatively constant level all year.

Below: **Most areas of Egypt still use age-old canals along with water wheels and motor driven pumps to irrigate farmlands. However, some of the new desert reclamation projects are using modern irrigation systems, such as sprinkle and pivotal irrigation or drip irrigation.**

One of the biggest problems that has occurred since Egypt switched to perennial irrigation is that the rich top soil that came from the floods is no longer in the water. The soil is now trapped behind the Aswan dams. To counteract the lack of new soil and more intensive agriculture, Egyptians have had to use more fertilizers and pesticides.

At this time, the Egyptian government is reconsidering which crops are best suited to little water and drought, expanding the use of sophisticated surface irrigation systems, and intensifying research on alternative water sources.

Joyful Occasions

Weddings are important occasions in Egypt, whether Muslim or Christian, rich or poor. Often an entire village or neighborhood is invited to the festivities, and the entertainment includes belly dancers, singers, and other performers.

Traditionally, a *waseet* (WAH-seet), or mediator, is sent by the father of the prospective husband to the girl's parents to seek their approval for a match. Following this confirmation, the fathers meet to work out the details.

On the engagement day, the groom's parents, friends, and family take presents to the bride's house. After everyone has eaten, the father of the future groom thanks the prospective bride's father for his hospitality and formally asks for the hand of his daughter. The prospective bride's father responds by saying the honor is his and that the visit has not been in vain. The formalities conclude when he shakes hands with the future groom and his father, and the groom places a wedding ring on his bride's and his own ring fingers.

Left: Urban weddings tend to be more elaborate than those in villages, but marriage is special regardless of where it takes place. At this city celebration, the bride is in a white, Western-style dress, and the reception is at a hotel. There will be belly dancers and other entertainers, as well as a lavish feast for the many friends and family who attend.

Other formalities include a marriage payment called a *mahr* (mah-HAHR), but no vows are exchanged between the bride and groom. At a later date, the legal representative of the bride and groom and two witnesses sign the marriage contract in the presence of the marriage registrar.

On the wedding day, the groom has a haircut and a bathing ceremony. After the groom's bath, his friends sing and give money to the barber for his role in the ceremony. Next, the groom and his friends walk in a procession to his parents' house.

Below: Newlyweds share a picnic. Families are important, and divorce is rare, particularly in rural areas where it would bring shame on both families. Both the Qur'an and the Bible discourage divorce.

The bride's bathing and beautification rites take place at her own home. The girl's friends sing, clap, and entertain the bride during the ceremony, while her family serves food, soft drinks, and tea.

When the bride is ready, the groom's family takes her and her family to their home. They walk in a procession, singing and dancing along the way. Sometimes a band leads the procession. Once there, the bride sits on a platform to be seen by all. The groom visits with her briefly, then joins his male guests in a separate room, while the bride is entertained by women.

The wedding night entertainment usually lasts until well after midnight. Then the groom goes to the newlyweds' room, where his bride has prepared food and is waiting for him.

Land of the Gods

The region known as Nubia is located in southern Egypt and northern Sudan. The banks of the Nile are narrow through much of old Nubia, which made farming difficult, but Nubians farmed, fished, and traded goods up and down the Nile River.

Nubia was important to Egypt because it was a source of precious metals and stones. It served as a trade corridor to Africa, and it was a source of manpower and labor. Nubia was a prosperous marketplace at the crossroads of ancient caravan routes. It also guarded Egypt from invasion from the south.

The earliest of the Nubian cultures was located in northern Nubia, in approximately 3800–3100 B.C. In the seventh century A.D., Nubia converted to Christianity. Islam did not reach the Nubian people until about 1400, much later than other parts of Egypt, because Nubian archers successfully repelled earlier Islamic invasions.

OLD NUBIA

Nubia was once known for its gold mines, ebony, ivory, and incense, all products highly valued by its neighbors. To the Greeks, Nubians were known as Ethiopians and the area as the Land of Ponts (Land of the Gods).

Below: Nubian villagers in Kom Ombo.

Above: **Nubian villagers use "cow power" to draw water from a well.**

In the early 1960s, the Aswan High Dam created Lake Nasser (300 miles/483 km long), which permanently flooded ancient temples and tombs, as well as Nubian land and hundreds of villages.

The flooding of the land, followed by moving to new villages, altered the Nubians' traditional way of life, which had existed virtually unchanged up to that time. Some Nubian men migrated to Cairo to work. Many entered the service industry and became well-known for their honesty and good character.

The Nubian populations were relocated north of Aswan, around the area of Kom Ombo. Since then, most have learned to speak Arabic, and many now intermarry with other Egyptians. Nubians are well on the way to dominating white-collar employment in Upper Egypt, and many Nubians have become quite wealthy on the relocated farmlands, where they specialize in sugarcane cultivation.

Culturally, the Nubians have lost their language, along with many traditional customs and ceremonies. However, the commercialization of dance and music for the tourists who visit Upper Egypt has provided not only a source of income, but also a means of keeping their traditions alive.

Peace with Israel

Negotiations for a permanent cease-fire between Israel and Egypt began in December 1973. Egypt and Israel signed agreements on January 18, 1974 and on September 1, 1975. Even so, in 1977, the outlook for peace between Egypt and Israel looked grim. Israel still held most of the Sinai, and negotiations had not moved forward since 1975. Israel's Prime Minister, Menachem Begin, was a hard-liner who supported Israeli expansionism.

President Anwar al-Sadat decided that something dramatic must be done. In a November address to the People's Assembly, Sadat said, "Israel will be astonished to hear me saying that I am ready to go to their own house, to the Knesset, itself, to talk to them." And he did, on November 19, 1977, in response to an invitation from Prime Minister Begin. Most of the world was amazed at Sadat's courage.

Most Egyptians favored his move, and even peace with Israel, if this would give them back their territories and lessen the burden of confrontation. Then, U.S. President Jimmy Carter invited Sadat and Begin to Camp David, near Washington, D.C.

Above: **Probably the most satisfying moment in President Jimmy Carter's term was when he helped to bring about peace between Egypt and Israel. Here, he clasps hands with President Sadat on the left and Prime Minister Begin on the right.**

The negotiations were tense and almost broke down. Finally, both sides reached an agreement, known as the Camp David Accords, on September 17, 1978. Six months later, on March 26, 1979, Egypt and Israel signed a peace treaty. Israel agreed to withdraw from the Sinai within three years. Normal diplomatic and trade relations were to be established between the two countries. Israeli ships would pass unhindered through the Suez Canal. However, Egypt would not have full sovereignty over the Sinai. A multinational observer force would be stationed in the Sinai, and the United States would monitor events there.

Below: **Peace at last. President Sadat** *(left, standing in car)* **celebrates the signing of the Camp David Accords with Israel.**

Sadat and Begin were heroes in the West, but Sadat was almost universally condemned by the Arab world. Many Arab countries severed diplomatic relations, suspended aid to Egypt, and expelled it from the Arab League and other Arab groups. The Arabs objected to the separate peace agreement, while Sadat insisted the treaty provided the basis for a more comprehensive settlement of the Arab–Israeli conflict. Arabs believed only a unified Arab stance and the threat of force would result in a solution. Also, without Egypt's military, no Arab country was strong enough to confront Israel. The Arab–Israeli conflict remained an unresolved, destabilizing force in the region.

Suez Canal

The Suez Canal is 100 miles (160 km) long — a man-made waterway connecting the Mediterranean Sea with the Red Sea. It opened in November 1869. The canal is economically and strategically important because it shortens the distance between Asia and Europe by over 5,000 miles (8,000 km). Before it was built, ships had to go all the way around Africa to get to India and the rest of Asia.

The canal was built and originally owned by British, French, and Egyptian interests, but Egypt's concessions to the building company proved very costly to the country. The Suez Canal Company was granted a strip of tax-free land to connect the Nile with the canal; thus Egypt gave up an important source of income and also had to provide the labor for building the canal.

During the years of the canal's construction, Egypt's rulers overspent and went into debt, which eventually resulted in their being forced to sell Egypt's share of the canal to Great Britain in 1875. The canal remained under British and French control until 1956.

AN ARAB HERO

The Suez crisis and President Nasser's firm stance over Egypt's control of the canal made him a hero in the Arab world. He became head of a pan-Arab nationalist movement that emphasized Arab unity.

Left: Egyptian soldiers watch a U.S. carrier pass through the Suez Canal waterway.

Fighting Over the Canal

In 1956, President Gamal Abdel Nasser, angry with Western powers that refused to provide funding for construction of the Aswan High Dam and also with Israel's February 1955 attack on Egyptian military outposts in Gaza, nationalized the Suez Canal. As a result, Israel attacked Egypt in October of the same year. Israel was supported by the British and the French, who were angry about the nationalization.

Both the United States and the Soviet Union put pressure on the invading nations and ended the so-called Suez War, leaving Nasser triumphant (despite his military losses) and the Suez Canal firmly in Egyptian hands. Although the Israelis did withdraw, they carried out a "scorched earth" policy, destroying roads, railroads, and military installations as they left. A United Nations Emergency Force (UNEF) was established, and peace-keeping troops remained until 1967.

Egypt reopened the canal in April 1957 but refused to allow Israeli shipping through it. During the Six-Day War (1967), Egypt sank ships to block the canal, and it remained closed until 1975. Israeli shipping rights were restored when Egypt and Israel signed a peace treaty on March 26, 1979.

Today, the canal is one of the world's busiest shipping lanes. Tankers carry petroleum, coal, metals and other goods to Europe, while others return to the Persian Gulf with cereal grains, fertilizers, fabricated metals, and cement.

Above: **Since 1975, the Suez Canal has been the busiest waterway in the world. Tankers carrying petroleum are among its main traffic.**

Suzanne Mubarak and Education

Helping Children Read

Mrs. Suzanne Mubarak, wife of President Hosni Mubarak, is "Mama Suzanne" to Egyptian children. She has played a socially active role in Egypt for many years, and children's education is dear to her heart. She is the founder and chairperson of the Integrated Care Society, a nonprofit organization that provides social, cultural, and health services for children. The society has set up children's libraries throughout the country. It also assists government school libraries and runs mobile and portable libraries that can travel from place to place.

Below: **Suzanne Mubarak has set up public libraries throughout Egypt for children and has started literacy programs to encourage reading and turn it into a lifetime habit.**

A Museum for Children

One of Mrs. Mubarak's ideas was to establish a museum primarily for children. The Suzanne Mubarak Museum for Children, inaugurated in 1996, stands in a forest park in Heliopolis, Cairo, surrounded by many plants and trees. The museum is designed to develop children's freedom to think, discover, and interact. They learn about Egypt's natural history and their cultural heritage and are encouraged to develop a concern for environmental protection. There are exhibits on the deserts of Egypt, as well as a Red Sea Hall, an Activity Center, and a Discovery Hall.

Above: **Mrs. Suzanne Mubarak *(center, left)* and President Hosni Mubarak *(center, right)* meet Britain's royal family. Mrs. Mubarak has won many international awards for her efforts to improve the quality of life of women and children in Egypt.**

A Better Life for All

Mrs. Mubarak has not confined her efforts to children alone. She has also launched a campaign to increase literacy among adults. Additional public libraries for adults have been set up, especially in low income areas. Much of her work is geared toward improving women's lives, in particular improving the health care and work possibilities available to them.

Taming the River

The Aswan High Dam is the second dam built to block the Nile in the vicinity of the first cataract (an area of rapids and waterfalls) at Aswan. The first dam (the Aswan Low Dam) was a granite dam constructed in three stages in 1902, 1912, and 1933. The low dam was designed to store water during the three-month flood season and to produce hydroelectric power, but it did not provide enough water or power for a population that grew from ten million in 1900 to twenty-six million in 1960. Egypt desperately needed to increase food production. Since only irrigated lands could be farmed, Egypt had to find a way to extend the farming season, increase the number of acres that could be farmed, or both. By building the High Dam at Aswan, Egypt sought to control all floods of the Nile, store water so there could be regulated releases throughout the year, and use released water to produce hydroelectric power.

Below: **The Aswan High Dam has a hydroelectric power capacity of 2.1 million kilowatts and supplies more than 25 percent of Egypt's power. It took ten years to build the dam, at a cost of one billion dollars.**

The Aswan High Dam was completed in 1970. One of the world's largest structures, it rises 364 feet (111 m) above the riverbed and is 2.3 miles (3.7 km) long. Construction of the dam created Lake Nasser, the world's largest man-made lake.

Both Aswan dams have caused concern in the archaeological world. Many ancient archaeological sites and treasures were in the path of rising lake waters behind the dam. Through heroic international efforts, Abu Simbel's great temple and colossi of Ramses the Great, which were going to be flooded, were actually cut into blocks, moved to the new lake shore, and reassembled. The Temple of Philae was also moved to higher ground.

Construction of the dam was not only a threat to Egypt's ancient heritage, but also to its people and environment. Many Nubians had to be moved to new villages north of Aswan. Bedouins also changed their seasonal migration patterns and now tend to stay in more settled communities along the lake shore. Damming the river also changed the environment downstream. Fewer nutrients reaching the Mediterranean Sea resulted in a drop in the fish catch. Fertile silt is now trapped behind the dam, and fertilizer use downriver has had to increase. Vegetation changed along the lake shores, and wild animals migrated to the area.

Above: **The dam opened more land for agriculture but decreased the amount of fertile silt that came every year with floods.**

SCHISTOSOMIASIS

A negative result of the taming of the Nile River has been the increase in a disease called schistosomiasis. A parasite transmitted by snails penetrates the human skin, usually through the foot, then travels through the blood vessels. Snails thrive in slow-moving water, and now that the Nile is dammed, the water flow is steady and there are no dry spells to keep the snail population down.

Tourists Are Big Business

Egypt capitalizes on its unique position in the history of the world by focusing tourist packages, videos, and advertising campaigns on its antiquities. As a result, tourism has become one of Egypt's most important economic resources. The number of tourists visiting Egypt rose from approximately 1.4 million in 1982 to nearly 4 million in 1996. In the 1994/95 fiscal year, tourism contributed $2.3 billion to Egypt's economy.

Tourists are typically in Egypt for only a short period of time. Most tour packages seem to have options ranging from five- to ten-day stays in Egypt, which means that tourists make only superficial contact with "real" Egyptian culture. Most people with whom tourists come in contact are either directly working in tourism, have a closely allied business, such as hotels or restaurants, or just happen to live or work in places that tourists visit.

Below: **Tourists ride camels beside the Red Sea. Arabian camels have one hump and are about 7 feet (2 m) tall at the shoulder. Their humps are made of fat, and they can go without food or water for several days at a time. Their wide-spread feet walk easily on the sand.**

The reverse is also true; Egyptians get to see tourists only in one light, that of people on vacation. Therefore, each sees the other from a very limited perspective and has little time to actually develop a long-standing social relationship. This short-term (and very limited) cultural interaction often leads to misunderstandings about what people are like in their respective cultures.

Tourists most often travel around Egypt in special air-conditioned tour buses. The bus is like a cocoon surrounding the tourists, so they rarely experience the smells, sounds, and feeling of being among the average population in Egypt. Tour guides are well trained. Many visitors take a Nile cruise on one of the large, first-class ships going up and down the river. When tourists visit a major tourist site, numerous small kiosks line the way to the entrance. Here the tourist can find almost any souvenir, from the very cheap to the moderately expensive. Tourists often refer to passing among these vendors as "running the gauntlet" because of the overwhelming crush of people shouting and trying to get their attention.

Above: **In bazaars like this one, tourists can find almost any kind of souvenir. Bazaars are where tourists first learn about the Egyptian art of bargaining. No vendor ever expects a person to pay the price he asks for merchandise. Instead, the shopper is expected to offer much less. Then a rapid exchange of counter-offers ensues until the two parties agree on an acceptable price.**

Urban Jungle

Egyptians use every means of transportation imaginable. Cairo, one of the world's largest cities, with 10 to 12 million people, has severe traffic congestion. The millions of cars on the streets, with no emission controls, result in stifling air pollution. Tahrir Square in central Cairo is like one gigantic, uncontrolled, moving mass. Eight wide streets, along with several alleys and parking areas feed its broad, center circle. Multi-storied shops, office buildings, hotels, and the Egyptian National Museum form the landscape around the square.

In the center of the square is a large green area with sidewalk vendors selling everything from cold drinks to tourist trinkets. Multitudes of people on foot and thousands of vehicles swarm through the streets. People are packed into buses, some hanging halfway out into the street.

Below: **A relatively quiet day in Tahrir Square, Cairo.**

Left: On buses and trains, women do not jam together with the men. They sit or stand only with other women. The new Metro actually has two separate cars reserved for women.

Pedestrians do not use designated crosswalks or even sidewalks necessarily. They cross streets from any point and form part of the whole interactive traffic pattern. They weave their way through as many as eight or ten widths of cars, buses, and trucks often moving in several directions and at varying speeds. There are also people on fast moving motorcycles or slow moving bicycles pedaled by delivery boys balancing huge trays of bread on their head. Some people hurry to catch one of the many buses at the central bus station. All kinds of buses stop at Tahrir Square: micro-buses, mini-buses, city buses, even tourist buses. Many taxis also pick up and deposit passengers in the vicinity of this central location, stopping anywhere they deem appropriate. No lanes or lights are observed. The rule of thumb is "just go if you can find space." Often a man on a donkey plods through the maze of human and vehicle traffic, calmly making his way to his destination.

Nearby is an entrance to Egypt's newest and most modern transportation system — the Metro, or subway, which connects some of the major areas of Cairo. Television screens showing comedies, commercials, or news entertain the passengers during the short wait between trains. No food, drinks, or smoking are allowed in the subway, and many uniformed police are on hand to ensure this policy is not violated.

RELATIONS WITH NORTH AMERICA

Egypt and North America have had close ties of friendship since 1973, when Egypt first began to negotiate for peace with Israel. Canada, the United States, and Egypt work closely together to promote peace and stability as well as economic prosperity in the Middle East. There are a number of business agreements between the countries, and the American Chamber of Commerce in Cairo represents both Egyptian and U.S. interests.

Opposite: Arabian horses have been bred for centuries in Egypt and are known for their great speed, beauty, and endurance. The horse in the movie, *The Black Stallion*, was probably born in Egypt.

The American Research Center in Egypt supports archaeological and academic research. It is partially funded by the U.S. Agency for International Development (USAID) and has financed thirty major conservation projects.

Americans tend to be fascinated by Egypt's rich history, while Egyptians are interested in modern technology and economic and social development. As a result, Egyptians tend to know much more about current trends in the United States than Americans know about modern Egypt.

Above: Kentucky Fried Chicken is a favorite fast-food outlet with Americans and Egyptians alike. This shop has the name in both English and Arabic.

History of Relations

Relations between Egypt and the United States and Canada have changed at different times during this century. Canada's government policies tend to be tied to those of Great Britain, and the United States has had a close alliance with Great Britain for a long time. The United States and Canada have not always agreed on every issue or detail, but they have, more often than not, adopted a unified position concerning Egypt.

Egypt was a protectorate of Great Britain from 1882 through 1952, although up to 1900, Egypt was, "in name," part of the Ottoman Empire. The Suez Canal was owned primarily by British and French interests, so Egypt was of strategic importance to the Allies in World War II, because whoever controlled the canal controlled access to Asia. Egypt saw repeated offensives by the Germans against the Allied forces.

After World War II, Egyptians sought freedom from British rule. They overthrew the British-supported monarchy in Egypt in 1952, and the country became an independent republic.

Below: **British tanks near Giza, just outside Cairo. The British armed forces were a presence in Egypt from 1882 to 1954, when the last soldier left.**

Break in Relations

Egypt was not happy with the establishment of the state of Israel by the West in 1948, yet a serious split between Egypt and the United States did not begin until February 1955 when the Israeli army attacked Egyptian military outposts in Gaza, killing thirty-nine Egyptians. President Gamal Abdel Nasser became convinced that Egypt must arm itself for defense against Israel. Although Egypt is a founding member of the Nonaligned Movement — countries that do not endorse either Western democracy or communist policies — Nasser sought aid from the United States. When the United States refused to sell arms to Egypt, Nasser turned to the communist bloc countries and bought arms from them.

Further exacerbating relations with the United States, Egypt's recognition of communist China led to a serious break in relations between Egypt and the United States. Although the United States had agreed to lend Egypt $56 million to build the Aswan High Dam, the offer was withdrawn. Nasser was furious, and, one week later on July 26, 1956, he nationalized the Suez Canal. Britain, France, and Israel tried to regain control of the canal but were condemned worldwide for taking action against Egypt.

Above: **President Mubarak** *(center)* **has sought to establish himself as an arbiter among Arab nations and is a leader in the Middle East peace process.**

THE COLD WAR

The Cold War grew out of distrust between the East and West after World War II. The Soviet Union, the "Iron Curtain" countries it controlled after the war, and China were communist countries. The United States, Canada, and most Western countries are democracies.

Tension Eases

In 1972, relations with the United States began to improve when President Anwar al-Sadat expelled Soviet advisors and began to seek closer ties with the West. Egypt's offensive against Israel in 1973 set those relations back, but Sadat's later determination to bring about a peace settlement with Israel was enthusiastically endorsed by the United States.

Following the cease-fire with Israel, U.S. diplomats began to negotiate with Egypt and Israel, shuttling back and forth between the Middle Eastern countries and the United States. Peace came with the signing of the Camp David Accords in 1979.

President Sadat's ties with the United States and his efforts toward peace with Israel undoubtedly contributed to his early death. Within Egypt, response to the treaty was generally favorable, but opposition arose from the left and from the Muslim Brotherhood, which has supporters in Egypt, northern Africa, and the Middle East. On October 6, 1981, Sadat was assassinated by members of a secret extremist group, al Takfir Wal Hijra (al-TAK-feer wal HIJ-ra, Repentance and Flight from Sin), as he reviewed a military parade on the eighth anniversary of the Suez crossing.

SHUTTLE DIPLOMACY

Between 1973 and 1978, Israel and Egypt negotiated for a permanent cease-fire. Much of the work was done by Secretary of State Henry Kissinger of the United States, during the Nixon administration, and Assistant Secretary of State Warren Christopher, during the Carter administration. They flew back and forth between Israel and Egypt so often that their negotiations were called Shuttle Diplomacy.

A Leader for Peace

Although many Egyptians were pleased to have peace with Israel, Egypt was ostracized by other Arab nations in the Middle East. Egypt was isolated from her neighbors for six years, until 1983, when President Hosni Mubarak met with Palestinian Liberation Organization (now Palestinian Authority) leader Yasser Arafat in Cairo. In January 1984, the Islamic Conference Organization unconditionally readmitted Egypt, and an Arab summit resolution in November 1987 allowed Arab countries to resume diplomatic relations with Egypt. Since then, Egypt has reestablished relations with other Arab countries and promoted Middle Eastern peace.

In the 1990s, Egypt's alliance with the United States and other Western countries in the Gulf War has enhanced the country's position as a reliable partner of the West but has led to internal dissidence because extremist groups do not want to compromise with the West. This conflict and several violent attacks against Westerners have affected both tourism and the economy.

President Mubarak has sought to establish a role for himself as arbiter with Arab nations of the region and as a leader in the Middle East peace process.

Above: Secretary of State Cyrus Vance of the United States *(left)* during the Carter administration and former Minister of State for Foreign Affairs Dr. Boutros Boutros-Ghali of Egypt *(right)*. Dr. Boutros-Ghali was secretary general of the United Nations from 1992 to 1996.

Opposite: U.S. fighter jets take part in joint military exercises with the Egyptian Armed Forces.

North Americans in Egypt

The precise number of North Americans in Egypt at any given time is not known because the number changes dramatically from day to day. Most North Americans go to Egypt as tourists. They tend to stay there for only a short time. Other Americans on short-term visits to Egypt are business people who go to establish business relationships or have business interests in Egypt, or are students at one of the many universities.

A small number of Americans may move to Egypt because they marry an Egyptian citizen and choose to live there either for some period of time or permanently.

There are also expatriate Americans in Egypt. People with businesses in the country may move their families with them and stay for several years.

Americans tend to live in the areas of Cairo where most other Americans live. Three favorite neighborhoods for Americans in Cairo are Maadi, Garden City, and Zamalek. These areas of town have many services and shops that cater to foreign interests, including foreign schools (American and British styles).

EXPATRIATES

Expatriates are people who live outside their own countries for an extended period of time. Sometimes they simply like the foreign country better than their home country, but usually, especially in the case of North Americans, expatriates go abroad for work or to study.

Left: **An outdoor café at the Marriott Hotel in Egypt. Visiting Americans quickly learn, especially over a leisurely meal, that Egyptians are wonderful hosts.**

Left: **McDonald's and Coca-Cola are two multinational companies that employ and train Egyptians.**

Egyptian Immigration to North America

Egyptians, like people everywhere, immigrate for many reasons. Most Egyptians who immigrate go to other Arab-speaking countries in the Middle East. Their purpose for immigrating is almost always for work. Most Egyptians who immigrate within the Middle East are skilled laborers and are well educated.

Egyptians tend to go to North America for either education or work. Those who immigrate to North America are almost always highly educated. Although Egypt has excellent universities, there are some specializations, for example in medicine, that are not available in Egypt. Others go for post-graduate training in areas for which the West is noted.

Among the people who migrate to North America for work, many are private business people who open businesses in towns where they locate. Others may be highly trained university professors or physicians.

YEAR IN CAIRO

Brown University in Providence, Rhode Island, offers both graduate and undergraduate degrees in Egyptology. Undergraduates may study in Cairo for their junior year abroad.

Where Do Egyptians Live in North America?

Although most live around major cities, such as Houston, New York, Los Angeles, Chicago, and Washington, D.C, Egyptians are spread out around most states in the United States. One interesting aspect about Egyptians who migrate is they do not generally move to "Egyptian" or "Middle Eastern" neighborhoods. More frequently, Egyptian families live in and among many neighborhoods and sectors of a city, rather than in geographically defined urban areas.

Current Relations with Egypt

Both Canada and the United States have many important programs of assistance to Egypt.

Egypt became eligible for Canadian assistance in 1976. Since that time it has ranked consistently among the main recipients of Canadian assistance. Aid from the Canadian International Development Agency (CIDA) is based on Egypt's need for development assistance, its support for the Middle East peace process, its stance as a moderate regime, and its potential as a market for Canadian exports and investments. CIDA's disbursements to Egypt in 1994–1995 totaled approximately $465 million.

Below: The American University in Cairo has educated students from around the world since it was established in 1923.

The United States disburses aid to Egypt through the U.S. Agency for International Development (USAID). Estimated U.S. support funds for Egypt in 1998 total $815,000,000.

Since the Camp David Accords in 1979, Egypt has used its leadership to foster a broader peace in the Middle East by developing and continuing to have good relations with its Arab neighbors. There is a yearly Middle East/North Africa economic summit where businesses and government leaders in the area plan economic reform and discuss ideas that will lead to peace and prosperity.

As a mechanism to promote stability and prosperity in Egypt, the U.S.–Egyptian Partnership for Economic Growth and Development was launched by Vice President Al Gore and Egyptian President Hosni Mubarak in September 1994. Both the United States and Egypt recognize that a prosperous and stable Egypt is vital for maintaining regional stability. The goals of the partnership are to: (1) promote economic growth and job creation, (2) increase the role of the private sector in the Egyptian economy, and (3) foster economic reform in Egypt. These goals reflect the views of both countries that economic opportunities and job creation are critical to long-term stability and the well-being of the Egyptian people.

Above: **A perfect example of combining East and West is the new Kasr el-Aini Teaching Hospital, which was designed and funded by the French but built by Egyptians. This building incorporates Egyptian lotus and papyrus motifs and the traditional use of marble along with modern Western building shapes and massive glass walls.**

Cultural Influences

Cultural influences have been almost entirely a one-way flow from the United States and Canada to Egypt. When Americans think of Egypt, it is almost always within the purview of ancient Egypt. Everyone in North America seems to be familiar with pyramids and sphinxes, but few Americans have adopted any aspects of Egyptian Islamic architecture, culture, clothing, or food. Most major cities have a few Middle Eastern or Greek restaurants, but these foods have not become part of the daily menu for most North Americans. Even Egyptian ethnic clothing and jewelry have not become popular in the United States, except for infrequent hieroglyphic designs on fabric.

The most significant American influence in Egypt is technology transfer. The first important cultural influence came from the radio. Next came television, but, for a long time, the government controlled the programming on state-owned stations. Once cable and satellite dishes began invading the landscape, Egyptians were no longer limited to seeing what the government approved. As a result, Egyptians are becoming more and more familiar with North American people as portrayed through film and television.

Below: **The Cairo Opera House has a museum, library, art gallery, music halls with great acoustics, and all the latest equipment. Both international and local groups make appearances at this well-known performing arts center.**

Left: **Belly dancing, an age-old Egyptian and Middle Eastern art form, is popular in the United States, especially in American colleges and exercise gyms. In Egypt, in fact, belly dancers are often American or Western women because many Egyptian women are too reserved to perform in scanty clothing.**

Access to the Internet was almost non-existent in 1994–95 but increased in 1996, and by the summer of 1997, there were cyber cafés in Cairo. Computers are still a luxury item, but the number of people with access increases daily.

American brand names in clothing are highly valued by young and wealthy middle-aged Egyptians. Western popular music plays in discos and on cruise ships, and Western foods and restaurants are growing in popularity, although they are mostly limited to the main cities.

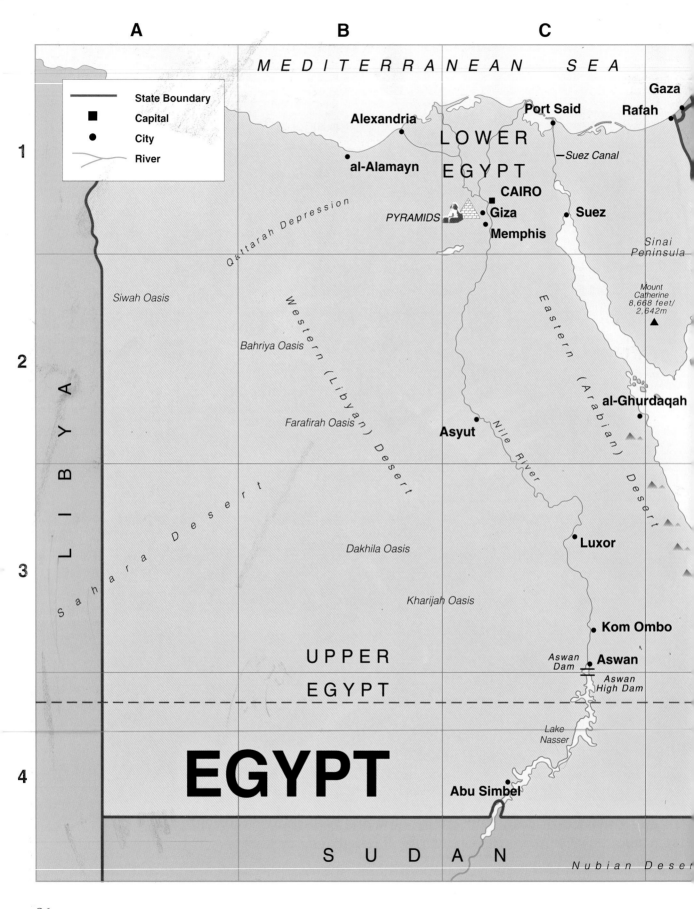

A　　　　　　**B**　　　　　　**C**

M E D I T E R R A N E A N   S E A

State Boundary		
■ Capital		
● City		
River		

Gaza

Port Said　　**Rafah**

Alexandria　　L O W E R

1　　　　　　●**al-Alamayn**　　E G Y P T　　—*Suez Canal*

CAIRO

■

PYRAMIDS　　●**Giza**　　●**Suez**

●**Memphis**

Sinai Peninsula

Siwah Oasis

▲ *Mount Catherine 8,668 feet/ 2,642m*

Qattarah Depression

Western (Libyan) Desert

Bahriya Oasis

2

Eastern (Arabian) Desert

Farafirah Oasis

●**al-Ghurdaqah**

●**Asyut**

Nile River

S a h a r a   D e s e r t

Dakhila Oasis

●**Luxor**

3

Kharijah Oasis

●**Kom Ombo**

U P P E R　　*Aswan Dam*　　●**Aswan**

E G Y P T　　*Aswan High Dam*

Lake Nasser

EGYPT

4

●**Abu Simbel**

L I B Y A

S U D A N

N u b i a n   D e s e r

D

West Bank
Jerusalem

N

JORDAN

SAUDI

ARABIA

R E D   S E A

Tropic of Cancer

Above: Sound and light show at Giza. In a deep voice, the Sphinx tells the story of the Great Pyramids.

Abu Simbel C4
al-Alamayn B1
al-Ghurdaqah C2
Alexandria B1
Aswan C3
Aswan Dam C3
Aswan High Dam C3
Asyut C2

Bahriya Oasis B2

Cairo C1

Dakhila Oasis B3

Eastern Desert C2

Farafirah Oasis B2

Gaza D1
Giza C1
Gulf of Aqaba D2
Gulf of Suez C2

Israel D1

Jerusalem D1
Jordan D1

Kharijah Oasis B3
Kom Ombo C3

Libya A1–A4

Lower Egypt B1–B2
Luxor C3

Mediterranean Sea B1–C1
Memphis C1
Mount Catherine D2

Nasser, Lake C4
Nile River C2–C3
Nubian Desert C4–D4

Port Said C1
Pyramids C1

Qattarah Depression B1

Rafah D1
Red Sea D3

Sahara Desert A4
Saudi Arabia D2
Sinai Peninsula C1–D1
Siwah Oasis A2
Sudan B4
Suez C1
Suez Canal C1

Upper Egypt B3–B4

West Bank D1
Western Desert B2

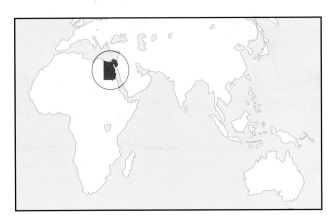

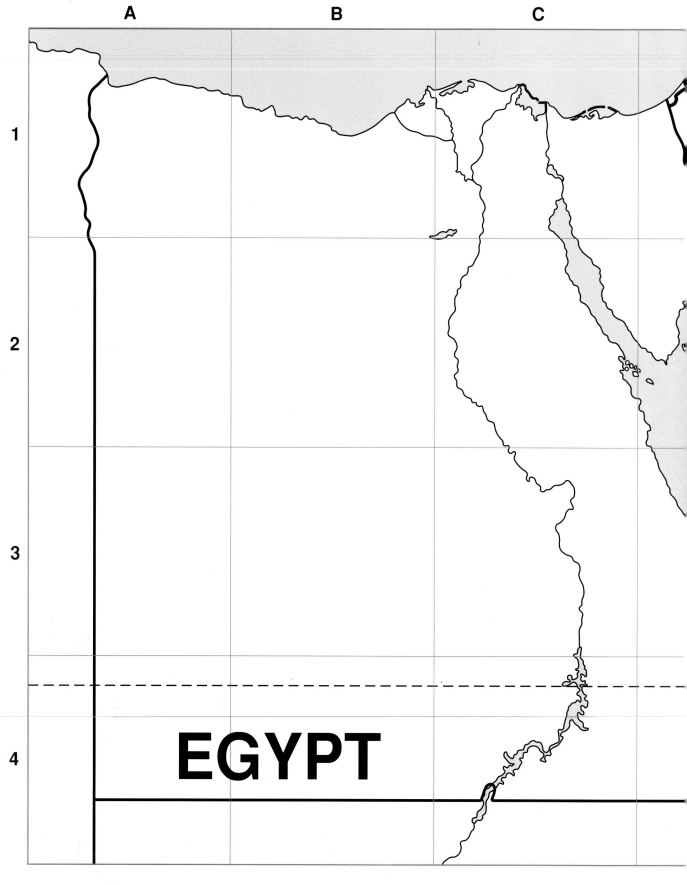

A B C

1

2

3

4

EGYPT

88

D

N

How Is Your Geography?

Learning to identify the main geographical areas and points of a country can be challenging. Although it may seem difficult at first to memorize the location and spelling of major cities or the names of mountain ranges, rivers, deserts, lakes, and other prominent physical features, the end result of this effort can be very rewarding. Places you previously did not know existed will suddenly come to life when referred to in world news, whether in newspapers, television reports, or other books and reference sources. This knowledge will make you feel a bit closer to the rest of the world, with its fascinating variety of cultures and physical geography.

Used in a classroom setting, the instructor can make duplicates of this map using a copy machine (PLEASE DO NOT WRITE IN THIS BOOK!). Students can then fill in any requested information on their individual map copies. Used one-on-one, the student can also make copies of the map on a copy machine and use them as a study tool. The student can practice identifying place names and geographical features on his or her own.

Below: **Philae Temple.**

Egypt at a Glance

Name of Country	Arab Republic of Egypt; Jumhuriyah Misr al-Arabiyah
Capital	Cairo
Official Language	Arabic
Population	63.6 million
Land Area	386,662 square miles (1,001,455 square kilometers)
Divisions	26 governorates
Highest Point	Mount Catherine (Jabal Katrina): 8,668 feet/2,642 m
Major River	Nile
Main Religion	Islam
Flag	Three equal horizontal bands of red (top), white, and black, with the national emblem centered in the white band.
National Emblem	A shield superimposed on a golden eagle facing the hoist side above a scroll bearing the name of the country in Arabic.
Government	Republic
Independence	February 28, 1922
National Holiday	Anniversary of the Revolution, July 23
Constitution	September 11, 1971
Legal System	Based on English common law, Islamic law, and Napoleonic codes.
Head of State	President Muhammad Hosni Mubarak
Famous Leaders	Muhammad 'Ali Pasha (1769–1849)
	Gamal Abdel Nasser (1918–1970)
	Anwar al-Sadat (1918–1981)
Birth Rate	2.9 percent
Literacy	51.4 percent
Currency	Egyptian pound (3.4 pounds = U.S. $1 as of 1998)

 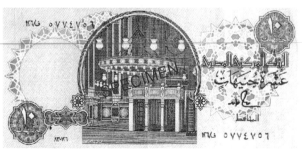

Opposite: **Pharaoh and Queen act out stories of ancient Egypt at Dr. Ragab's Pharaonic Village near Cairo.**

Glossary

Egyptian Vocabulary

ahlan wa sahlan (AH-lan was-AH-lan): welcome.

Allah (AHL-lah): God.

Amun (AH-moon): the sun god in ancient Egypt.

Bedouin (BED-oo-in): a nomadic Arab living in Egypt, North Africa, and the Arabian Peninsula.

Eid el-Adha (EYE-eed el-AD-hah): the big feast; celebration of the willingness of Abraham to sacrifice his son to God.

Eid el-Fitr (EYE-eed el-FIT-er): the little feast; celebration at the end of Ramadan.

felafel (fey-LAH-fal): fried balls of chickpeas and wheat; same as *ta'miya*.

fellahin (FELL-ah-heen): peasant farmer.

felucca (feh-LUKE-kah): a narrow wooden sailboat used in Egypt.

foul (FOOL): fava beans.

galabea (GAHL-ah-BAY-yah): a loose, ankle-length, traditional garment worn by men and women.

iftar (IFF-tar): literally, "break the fast." Meal taken after sunset during the month of Ramadan to break the fast.

imam (EE-mahm): a religious leader.

khamsin (KAHMA-SEEN): a very hot, dry wind with sandstorms during April and May.

maalesh (MAH-lesh): never mind.

mahr (mah-HAHR): a marriage payment by the groom's father to the bride's father.

moulid (MOO-led): birthday of a prophet or saint.

Moulid el-Nabi (MOO-led el-NAH-bi): festival celebrating the birth of Prophet Muhammad.

muezzin (MUH-a-zin): the person who calls people to prayer in Islam.

Nubians (NOO-be-an): dark-skinned Egyptians from the southern part of the country.

Qur'an (KOUR-aan): the holy book of Islam, also called the Koran.

Ramadan (RA-ma-DAAN): the holy month of fasting for Muslims.

sahour (sa-HOO-ur): the meal taken before dawn during Ramadan.

Shaaban (SHA-AB-an): the eighth month of the Islamic calendar.

Sham el-Nessim (SHAHM el-NESS-sem): Scent of Spring; a spring festival that dates back to the time of the pharaohs. It is celebrated on Easter Monday.

ta'miya (ta-MEE-ya): fried balls of chickpeas and wheat.

wadi (WAD-ee): dry streambed.

waseet (WAH-seet): mediator.

English Vocabulary

abolished: finished, gotten rid of.

alliance: various people or groups united in a common cause.

Apostles: the original twelve disciples called by Jesus to preach his gospel.

assassinate: to kill by secret attack.

barren: no vegetation.

bazaar: marketplace.

calligraphy: beautifully written words or characters, often done with brush strokes.

cataract: an area of rapids and waterfalls in a river.

confiscate: to seize; to take.

Copts: Christians in Egypt.

dam: barrier to obstruct the flow of water.

delta: fan-shaped area of land that forms at the mouth of a river.

dialect: a variety of a language that differs from the standard language used.

dynasty: a succession of rulers of the same line of descent.

economy: management and productivity of resources.

fast: (v.) to abstain from eating.

financial aid: help with money through gifts or loans.

hieroglyphics: a script that uses symbolic pictures to depict words.

Hittites: a group in central Anatolia that was powerful from 1900 to 1200 B.C.

irrigation: the practice of artificially supplying water to land by building canals or dikes.

kiosk: small stand that sells food, gifts, or souvenirs.

Lent: the Christian period of penitence and fasting during the forty days before Easter.

literate: able to read and write.

Lower Egypt: northern Egypt.

Mamluks: Turkish slaves who served in the Arab army. They took power and established their own dynasty from 1250 to 1517.

migrate: move from one place to another.

monastery: a community of monks or the place where a community of people has taken religious vows.

mosque: the place Muslims go to worship.

Muslim: a person who practices the faith of Islam.

nationalize: takeover of a place or an organization by the government.

oasis: a fertile spot in the desert watered by a spring, stream, or well.

obelisk: an upright pillar that tapers as it rises and ends in a pyramid on top.

occupied territories: areas taken over by Israel after the war of 1967. They included historic Palestine, the West Bank, the Gaza Strip, part of the Sinai, and the Golan Heights in Syria.

papyrus: tall, aquatic reed or paper made from the stems of the reed.

pharaoh: Egyptian king.

polytheism: a belief in many gods. Ancient Egyptians were polytheists.

prestige: reputation from successful achievements or from rank or other attributes.

protectorate: a country or person protected and partly controlled by a stronger person or country.

schistosomiasis: a tropical disease caused by a parasite, called a schistosome, that is carried by snails in slow-moving water.

sedentary: characterized by inactivity, staying in one place.

Shura: the Consultative Council to the Egyptian legislature.

sovereignty: supreme rule.

stalemate: a situation in which no action can be taken or progress made.

Upper Egypt: southern Egypt.

vendor: a person or stand that sells something, such as food.

Wafd: the organization that pressed for Egyptian independence from Britain.

More Books to Read

Ancient Egypt. Cultural Atlas for Young People series. Geraldine Harris (Equinox)

Ancient Egypt. Eyewitness Books series. George Hart (Dorling Kindersley)

Ancient Egypt. Make it Work! series. Andrew Haslam and Alexandra Parsons (Thomson Learning)

Cat Mummies. Kelly Trumble (Clarion Books)

Cleopatra. World Leaders Past and Present series. Dorothy Hoobler and Thomas Hoobler (Chelsea House Publishers)

Egypt. Festivals of the World series. Elizabeth Berg (Gareth Stevens)

The Egyptians. Pictures of the Past series. Denise Allard (Gareth Stevens)

Into the Mummy's Tomb: The Real-Life Discovery of Tutankhamun's Treasures. Nicholas Reeves (Madison Press)

Pyramids. Anne Millard (Larousse Kingfisher Chambers)

Tales of Ancient Egypt. Roger Lancelyn Green and Heather Copley (Puffin)

Videos

Egypt: Quest for Immortality. (Time-Life Video and Television)

Mummies: Tales from the Egyptian Crypts. (A&E Home Video)

The Pyramids and the Cities of the Pharaohs. (Questar Video)

The Tomb of Tutankhamun. (AIMS Media)

Web Sites

members.aol.com/mumifyddog/main.html

interoz.com/egypt/kids/History.htm

www.idsc.gov.eg/

pharos.bu.edu/Egypt/Home.html

Due to the dynamic nature of the Internet, some web sites stay current longer than others. To find additional web sites, use a reliable search engine with one or more of the following keywords to help you locate information on Egypt. Keywords: *Cairo, Egypt, Egyptians, Nubians, pyramids, Suez Canal.*

Index